THE BEDFORD SERIES IN HISTORY AND CULTURE

Power and the Holy in the Age of the Investiture Conflict

A Brief History with Documents

Related Titles in
THE BEDFORD SERIES IN HISTORY AND CULTURE
Advisory Editors: Lynn Hunt, *University of California, Los Angeles*
David W. Blight, *Yale University*
Bonnie G. Smith, *Rutgers University*
Natalie Zemon Davis, *Princeton University*
Ernest R. May, *Harvard University*

THE BEDFORD SERIES IN HISTORY AND CULTURE

Power and the Holy in the Age of the Investiture Conflict

A Brief History with Documents

Maureen C. Miller

University of California, Berkeley

BEDFORD/ST. MARTIN'S   Boston ◆ New York

For Bedford/St. Martin's

Executive Editor for History: Mary V. Dougherty
Director of Development for History: Jane Knetzger
Developmental Editor: Katherine A. Retan
Editorial Assistants: Shannon Hunt, Carina Schoenberger
Senior Production Supervisor: Nancy Myers
Senior Marketing Manager: Jenna Bookin Barry
Project Management: Books By Design, Inc.
Text Design: Claire Seng-Niemoeller
Indexer: Books By Design, Inc.
Cover Design: Billy Boardman
Cover Art: King Dagobert Invests Saint Omer. MS 698 folio 7. Courtesy of the
 Bibliothèque de l'agglomération de St-Omer.
Composition: Stratford Publishing Services, Inc.
Printing and Binding: Haddon Craftsmen, an RR Donnelley & Sons Company

President: Joan E. Feinberg
Editorial Director: Denise B. Wydra
Director of Marketing: Karen Melton Soeltz
Director of Editing, Design, and Production: Marcia Cohen
Manager, Publishing Services: Emily Berleth

Library of Congress Control Number: 2004109152

Manufactured in the United States of America.

0   9   8   7
f   e   d   c

For information, write: Bedford/St. Martin's, 75 Arlington Street, Boston, MA 02116
(617-399-4000)

ISBN-10: 0-312-40468-9 (paperback)
     1-4039-6806-3 (hardcover)
ISBN-13: 978-0-312-40468-0 (paperback)
     978-1-4039-6806-7 (hardcover)

Acknowledgments

Acknowledgments and copyrights are continued at the back of the book on pages
179–80, which constitute an extension of the copyright page.

To two teachers who changed my life:

Terence R. Murphy
Les Kaye

Foreword

The Bedford Series in History and Culture is designed so that readers can study the past as historians do.

The historian's first task is finding the evidence. Documents, letters, memoirs, interviews, pictures, movies, novels, or poems can provide facts and clues. Then the historian questions and compares the sources. There is more to do than in a courtroom, for hearsay evidence is welcome, and the historian is usually looking for answers beyond act and motive. Different views of an event may be as important as a single verdict. How a story is told may yield as much information as what it says.

Along the way the historian seeks help from other historians and perhaps from specialists in other disciplines. Finally, it is time to write, to decide on an interpretation and how to arrange the evidence for readers.

Each book in this series contains an important historical document or group of documents, each document a witness from the past and open to interpretation in different ways. The documents are combined with some element of historical narrative—an introduction or a biographical essay, for example—that provides students with an analysis of the primary source material and important background information about the world in which it was produced.

Each book in the series focuses on a specific topic within a specific historical period. Each provides a basis for lively thought and discussion about several aspects of the topic and the historian's role. Each is short enough (and inexpensive enough) to be a reasonable one-week assignment in a college course. Whether as classroom or personal reading, each book in the series provides firsthand experience of the challenge—and fun—of discovering, recreating, and interpreting the past.

Lynn Hunt
David W. Blight
Bonnie G. Smith
Natalie Zemon Davis
Ernest R. May

Preface

The purpose of this book is to update the presentation of an important historical event—the investiture conflict of the eleventh century—to help a new audience understand its enduring significance. The struggle was not just a political debate among elites about royal power; it was the product of movements for reform that transformed European society. By telling the story of the dramatic clash between Pope Gregory VII and Emperor Henry IV in this broader context, I hope to provide both instructors and students with materials to investigate the relationship between politics and religion, power and the holy, in their own cultures and in those of the past.

The volume will be most useful in two kinds of courses. The first is the survey of Western Civilization. The Middle Ages is often an uncomfortable way station in such a course, sandwiched between the emergence of ancient political systems and the decapitation of divine right monarchs in early modern England and France. This book explains how the Middle Ages created a distinctive and tenacious set of beliefs about sacred kingship which drew on late Roman political traditions and Christianity. It is designed to get students from the world of the Roman Empire to the world of Machiavelli, the Reformation, and the English Civil War.

This volume will also serve as a useful text in the medieval survey course. Instructors have long relied on Brian Tierney's *The Crisis of Church and State* to introduce students to the investiture conflict. Indeed, Tierney's seminal volume offers students fundamental sources in the intellectual, legal, and institutional history of medieval Europe. Most medievalists, however, are now uncomfortable with the application of the church/state framework to the eleventh century, since the emergence of something approximating a state is a story that belongs to the twelfth and thirteenth centuries. Most of their students, moreover, do not have the knowledge of Christianity that Professor Tierney could assume when he compiled his classic volume forty years ago. This book aims to explain the investiture conflict to students coming from diverse religious backgrounds who have been raised on social and cultural history.

The volume begins with an introduction that sets out the key events of the investiture conflict, explains what investiture meant to eleventh-century people, and places the struggle in a broad historical context, framing it in terms of a gradual shift in medieval conceptions of the nature of power and the holy. The introduction reaches back to the Roman Empire to trace the origins of sacred rulership in the West, describes the Christian appropriation of these ideas, and explains the emergence of the papacy in Rome—all of which led to the development of a potent model of sacred kingship in the early Middle Ages with the Carolingian dynasty. It locates the origins of the investiture conflict in the turbulent breakup of the Carolingian empire, explaining how insecurity in an age of political conflict and invasions affected the church and society.

The documents in Part Two allow students to place the investiture conflict within the broader context of social and political change in medieval Europe, and demonstrate the ways in which power and the holy became inextricably linked in this period. The documents in chapter 1 show how disorder spawned numerous movements for reform. Three issues that came to the fore—clerical celibacy, simony, and "free" election of bishops—are explained in their social and religious contexts. Chapter 2 traces how all these concerns, particularly those about the election of bishops, led to political crisis and war. The classic exchange of letters between Pope Gregory VII and Henry IV is recontextualized through the addition of alternate versions of events that bring out the complexity of both the issues and the personalities that divided Europe. Chapter 3 sketches the enormous changes over the twelfth and thirteenth centuries that the reform movements and the investiture crisis launched. The most important were a revolution in lay spirituality, the emergence of papal monarchy, and the intensification of royal claims to holiness by kings and their supporters.

Document headnotes provide students with the context necessary to understand and critique the evidence. Contrasting versions of events are provided by juxtaposing different accounts, and the Questions for Consideration at the end of the volume call students' attention to different points of view, contested issues, and broad themes. Visual learners will find images that enable them to analyze the representation of power and the holy in medieval Europe. A detailed chronology and maps are also provided to aid students in understanding the conflict,

while a bibliography supplies resources in English for further explo-
ration and study.

A NOTE ABOUT THE TEXTS AND TRANSLATIONS

In preparing this volume, I concentrated on recontextualizing the
"classic" works of the investiture conflict that have long been available
in translation by placing them in a much broader historical landscape.
Thus, this book is a blend of old and new. All translations of texts are
my own, except where indicated. In my new translations, I have tried
to make the complex Latin of eleventh-century churchmen accessible
to undergraduate readers by breaking down sentences and eliminat-
ing some verbal flourishes. For the same reason, I decided to reprint
Ephraim Emerton's translations of Gregory VII's letters rather than
H. E. J. Cowdrey's new edition (see bibliography). Cowdrey's translations more faithfully render Gregory's Latin syntax and phraseology.
Instructors and advanced students should consider them.

ACKNOWLEDGMENTS

A Mathy Fellowship from George Mason University supported the ini-
tial phases of editing and translating these documents, and I thank my
colleagues in the Western Civilization program at GMU—especially
T. Mills Kelly, Jack Censer, and Marion Deshmukh—for inspiring me
to think deeply about the place of the Middle Ages in Western history.
The generosity and wisdom of many colleagues improved this volume:
my thanks to series editor Lynn Hunt, University of California, Los
Angeles; Barbara H. Rosenwein, Loyola University of Chicago; Bruce
L. Venarde, University of Pittsburgh; Uta-Renate Blumenthal, Catholic
University of America; William North, Carleton College; R. I. Moore,
University of Newcastle upon Tyne; Sherri Olson, University of
Connecticut; Megan McLaughlin, University of Illinois at Urbana–
Champaign; and Louis A. Okin, Humboldt State University. I am grateful to Jane Knetzger and Mary Dougherty at Bedford / St. Martin's for
their support, and to Emily Berleth and Nancy Benjamin for guiding
the book through production. My editor, Kathy Retan, provided astute
suggestions to transform a behemoth manuscript into a volume, as well
as sage advice on so many matters. The errors and wayward opinions
remaining, of course, are my own.

Maureen C. Miller

Contents

Maps and Illustrations

PART ONE

Introduction: The Investiture Conflict in Western History

It was no wonder that if one household was entirely faithful, another was wholly unfaithful, and in a third a mother and child were believing, while a father and another child were unbelieving. Thus, the entire city was full of disorder and divided by conflict.[1]
— Andrew of Strumi, ca. 1075

Our island has not yet repudiated the one nor decided whether to obey the other. When the case for both sides has been heard (if that should happen), it will be possible to see more clearly what is to be done.   — Archbishop Lanfranc of Canterbury
to Hugh Candidus, 1085 (Document 27)

In the late eleventh century, a movement for reform within the western church led to a dramatic conflict between its leader, Pope Gregory VII, and the foremost sovereign in Europe, Emperor Henry IV. Called the investiture conflict (or the investiture "struggle" or "crisis"), this battle between the pope and the emperor divided the continent for decades. The flashpoint came in 1076 when Henry IV withdrew allegiance from the pope. Gregory responded by excommunicating Henry, declaring him deposed, and urging his subjects to rise up against him. They did, plunging the empire into civil war. As Pope Gregory was traveling north to meet with Henry's opposition and

1

elect a new king, the monarch intercepted him at the castle of Canossa in northern Italy. In a dramatic and desperate gesture, Henry stood barefoot in the snow outside the castle walls for three days, garbed as a penitent, stripped of all the trappings of royalty, begging to be reconciled with the church. Gregory absolved him, but the enraged opposition to Henry went ahead and elected an antiking, Rudolf of Swabia. The war ground on. In 1080 Pope Gregory renewed his excommunication of Henry because he continued to invest bishops. The monarch, in turn, withdrew allegiance from the pope and sponsored the election of an antipope (Clement III). That fall, Henry defeated the antiking Rudolf and then took his army to Rome. He chased Gregory from the city and had Clement III enthroned as pope. Even after Gregory died in exile in 1085, the conflict continued; it outlived Henry, too. Only in 1122 did a set of agreements reached at Worms in the German empire officially end the investiture conflict.

The issues raised by the reform movement that fueled this conflict elicited strong feelings: As Andrew of Strumi recorded, they polarized neighbors and even divided families in Milan. In the broader arena of European politics, the conflict between pope and emperor posed difficult, if not impossible, choices. Even the most educated observers, like Archbishop Lanfranc (Document 27), found that the complex issues, actions, and personalities involved made simple or decisive responses difficult.

The "case for both sides" that Lanfranc wanted heard has in fact been debated for nine centuries.[2] The polemics began in his own time, and some historians have carried them down to the present. The longevity of the debate and its capacity to polarize are due to the centrality of the forces involved: power and the holy. These forces are still related in our own political culture—a point I will return to at the end of this introduction—but they seemed impossible to disentangle in the eleventh century. The investiture conflict was the first attempt to sort them out. It was messy—war usually is—and tragically unsuccessful in the short run. But it shaped European politics for centuries, and the questions it raised at the time have reverberated down to the present.

POWER AND THE HOLY ON THE EVE OF THE INVESTITURE CONFLICT

The Ritual of Investiture

So what was investiture, and why did medieval Europeans feel so strongly about it? Investiture was a simple but visually memorable ritual of bestowing power. Lords, for example, invested vassals with fiefs. To understand this act, it is best to put aside our modern notions about property; investiture was not the medieval equivalent of a real estate "closing." It was about power, not ownership. The lord was granting power over both a piece of land and the people on it. The act also established a relationship of power: The giver was more powerful than the receiver. Both the character of the relationship and the transfer of power were made visible during the ceremony. Posture communicated the inequality of power: The lord was standing, the vassal kneeling. The handing over of symbolic objects effected the transfer of power. The choice of objects richly illustrates the complexity of the act. Although clods of earth, representing the land of the fief, might be handed over, usually a sort of stick or baton was passed from the hand of the lord to that of the vassal. In the Middle Ages, a staff or baton symbolized authority. The scepter was the royal version, whereas a lance or flag might be used for vassals. The latter symbolized power as well as the military service owed to the lord granting the fief. This ceremony of investiture, this series of memorable actions, was what counted—it effected the change. A document might record it, but if the transaction were challenged in the eleventh century, the document would have been used to call together those who had witnessed the ceremony. The memory of the witnesses—their testimony as to what they had seen—was probative; the document was not. Ritual mattered in the eleventh century; it created relationships and effected changes.

Bishops, the local leaders of Christian communities (or dioceses), also underwent this ritual of investiture—and it is this particular type of investiture that divided Europe at the end of the eleventh century. During this investiture, the bishop received the ring that symbolized his marriage to his "see" (his diocese or church) and the crosier, a staff similar to a shepherd's crook, that symbolized his authority and the pastoral care he exercised over his flock. Both objects were regarded as holy. The powers bishops exercised, moreover, were sacred: They could consecrate churches and ordain priests. But they were also profane: Bishops were great lords, controlling whole regions, and they were often royal vassals. Thus, over the early Middle Ages (ca. 500–1000), kings had become accustomed to investing bishops. Reformers in the eleventh century were scandalized by this custom and wanted it stopped. The question of *who* invested the bishop was critical: The investor was in the position of power and was seen as its source. The person who handed the sacred objects to the bishop was bestowing not just symbols but the power they represented as well. And just as feudal investiture articulated a relationship, so too did the investiture of a bishop. If a king invested him, a bishop was the king's man, exercising the authority of his office on behalf of the monarch.

The conflict that ensued hinged on the status of kings. Were they ordinary men wielding temporal power, or were they divinely ordained authorities ruling in God's name here on earth? This quickly widened into a broader debate over the origins and nature of both power and holiness. Where exactly did power come from? Did God grant it, or did men create it? What was holy? Can things be holy, or just people? How is holiness conferred or manifested? Can power in this fallen world be holy? Such questions related directly to the right-ordering of society and its governance. If holy power, spiritual power, is greater than worldly power, is the pope's power by nature greater than the emperor's?

Temporal versus Divine Authority

The relationship between holiness and worldliness, between sacred and profane, was not very clear on the eve of the investiture conflict, as can be seen in the distinctions drawn between "clergy" and "laity." Derived from the Greek *laos,* meaning "the people," the term *laity* generally was used to designate the body of the faithful. The clergy, by contrast, were those ordained in the service of the church, but there were various grades of clergy. The lesser or minor orders were doorkeeper, reader, exorcist, and acolyte. "Ordination" to these was effected either by a simple blessing or by investing the candidate with the instruments used in his office, such as a church key for a doorkeeper or a book for a reader. The major orders of subdeacon, deacon, and priest were conferred by the imposition of hands, a practice noted in the Acts of the Apostles (6:6) and believed to confer grace (2 Tim. 1:6). All members of the clergy were tonsured—that is, the tops of their heads were shaved—so they would be visually distinguishable from the laity. To complicate matters, however, monks also received the tonsure but were considered to be laypeople. The fact that they took vows and had abandoned "the world"—even though they were not ordained—led some observers to classify them separately. Indeed, the Benedictine abbot Abbo of Fleury in 999 distinguished three "orders": "The first is that of the laity, the second that of the clergy, the third that of the monks."[3] During the eleventh and twelfth centuries, it became more common for monks to receive clerical orders, many becoming priests, and this tended to assimilate the monastic and clerical "orders."

The status of kings was even less clear. From the early Middle Ages, kingship was seen as an office held by the grace of God. The election and coronation of kings, moreover, employed places, actions, objects, and substances used in other sacraments of the church. Coronations took place in church. In the West Frankish ritual, the king, just like a bishop, received a ring and a staff while prayers were said. And kings, like priests, were anointed with holy oil.[4] Blessed oil was believed to impart holiness. In the book of Exodus, God instructed Moses to "prepare sacred anointing oil, a perfume compounded by the perfumer's art. This shall be the sacred anointing oil. Anoint with it the Tent of the Presence and the Ark of the Tokens, the table and all its vessels. . . . You shall consecrate them, and they shall be most holy" (Exod. 30:25–29). God told Moses to consecrate Aaron and his sons as priests: "Their anointing shall inaugurate a hereditary priesthood for all time" (Exod. 40:12–15). The anointing of kings made them like priests. Contemporaries, however, were well aware of ways they differed from priests: They could not consecrate things or people, and they were not expected to be celibate.

During the reform movement, the special qualities and powers of the priesthood were strongly emphasized. This had the effect of demoting the minor orders of the clergy to a quasi-lay status. The holiness of kings was more directly and fiercely attacked. Reformers forcefully asserted that kings were only men like all men, but their contemporaries seem not to have followed their lead. Indeed, the most significant short-term result of the investiture conflict was that kings and their supporters renewed and intensified royal claims to holiness. This is why, centuries later, many European countries were still ruled by "divine right" monarchs. But kings were not the only ones to emerge from the conflict intransigent. Popes and their supporters not only continued to claim primacy over temporal rulers, but actually developed the power to back up these claims in certain instances. Over the rest of the Middle Ages, kings and popes continued to clash. Repeated conflict and independent institutional development did lead to a growing sense of separation between church and "state," but even at the close of the Middle Ages power and the holy were intimately related.

Power and the Holy versus Church and State

This volume focuses on power and the holy rather than invoking the more familiar dichotomy of "church" and "state" for a number of reasons. First, eleventh- and twelfth-century Europe did not really have "states." This term suggests a degree of organization that would have been unimaginable in the central Middle Ages. The dominant political form in the period of the investiture conflict was dynastic monarchy. Kings ruled through their physical presence and personal relationships—not through a bureaucratic administration—and this meant that they were constantly moving through their territories in order to renew alliances with local elites by means of gifts and threats. Those local potentates might be laymen, but they were just as frequently bishops, which brings us to a second reason to renounce the term "state" in favor of "power." Our notion of "state" implies "civil" or "secular" governance, yet in the eleventh and twelfth centuries, many activities that we consider proper to the "state"—such as the collection of taxes, the administration of justice, and the waging of war— were exercised by ecclesiastical leaders.

Finally, framing our inquiry in terms of power and holiness enables us to think about both the past and the present in more nuanced ways. While some nations today embrace the concept of church-state separation, the exercise of power is still tinged with references to the holy. Every president of the United States takes the oath of office with one hand on a Bible, and public officials frequently invoke a deity ("God bless America") at civic events. And while individuals holding public office are not believed to be holy, the office itself and the things associated with it may be said to be "desecrated" by certain types of actions. In sum, by focusing on the relationship between power and the holy in considering the Middle Ages, we not only avoid anachronism, but we gain perspective on our own political culture.

POWER AND THE HOLY
BEFORE THE MILLENNIUM

To appreciate the close interrelationship between power and the holy on the eve of the investiture conflict and the radical nature of many of the ideas it generated, a broad chronological perspective is necessary. Medieval Europe inherited varied practices and ideas about holiness and the exercise of authority from three traditions: the Roman Empire, Christianity, and the Germanic peoples who migrated into Western Europe beginning in the third century. The ideas and practices of each of these traditions contributed to the emergence in the late eighth and early ninth centuries of a new set of ideals about kingship that strongly influenced the development of the West.

The Late Roman Empire and Christianity

Our story, therefore, begins in the Roman Empire. Large parts of Europe had been incorporated into the empire, and so Roman culture was broadly diffused in the world that would become medieval. It was, however, specifically a late Roman imperial culture that was bequeathed to Europe, one in which emperors were both priests and gods. The image of the emperor that the colonized peoples in Europe and throughout the Mediterranean knew was the product of a complex and dramatic historical development. As the city-state of Rome conquered territories, it had to improvise means of ruling them. Its own republican political institutions proved inadequate: The Republic collapsed in 27 B.C.E. after decades of spectacular and destructive civil wars. It was replaced by the autocratic rule of one man: the emperor.

Historians once attributed the success of imperial rule to the development of a vast bureaucratic apparatus that united and pacified the far-flung territories subjected to Roman power. As researchers have looked more closely at the operation of Roman rule in the provinces, however, they have come to attribute its success more to astute alliances and cultural practices than to administrative domination. Particularly important were cultural practices that fostered allegiance, especially the careful propagation of an imperial image of sacrificial piety and heroic might. Augustus and his successors not only led a self-conscious revival of Roman religious practices, but also claimed for themselves multiple priestly offices formerly spread among elites. The image of the emperor as a veiled priest offering sacrifice was widely diffused in the provinces through statues, reliefs, and coins. The visual juxtaposition of these images with civic projects linked sacred rulership to the tangible benefits of imperial generosity: buildings, roads, and the prosperity brought by trade.[5] Thus, sacred rulership was key to Rome's success in dominating its empire.

Christianity at first registered hostility and ambivalence toward this construction of rulership, and because Christians refused to sacrifice to imperial images, Roman officials considered them traitors and persecuted them. But the Roman themes of divinity and sacrifice also infuse early Christian texts. Jesus of Nazareth, believed to be the son of God, takes on human flesh and then sacrifices himself for the salvation of humanity. In the Gospel of John (18:33–36), when a Roman official asks Jesus if he is king of the Jews, he responds, "My kingdom does not belong to this world." Other passages from the New Testament (Matt. 22:15–21; Rom. 13:1–7) also suggest a heavenly kingdom distinct from worldly political structures, but they counsel submission to earthly authorities. Thus, there was an important ambivalence in the teaching of Christianity. On the one hand, temporal authority was seen as part of the fallen, sinful world. On the other, it was seen as divinely ordained in God's plan for human salvation and so commanded acceptance and obedience.

When Christianity became the only licit religion in the Roman Empire in the fourth century, the image of the emperor as priest and god changed—but not as radically as one might think. The emperor Constantine began this process by converting to Christianity and making the religion legal (313); the Edict of Theodosius in 391 completed it by banning all other faiths. Constantine exercised roles—such as calling church councils and defining doctrine—that had previously been performed only by bishops. The divine ordination of the emperor's rule was emphasized, and a parallelism between the heavenly and earthly kingdoms was established. Just as God ruled over the divine world, the emperor governed this one: The emperor was God's representative on earth. Christian emperors continued the traditional role of being generous patrons to local communities, building churches and maintaining the fabric of urban life. Indeed, by the sixth century, imperial power had the aura of the holy. In Ravenna, the emperor Justinian and empress Theodora were depicted bringing the Eucharistic sacrificial offerings to the altar, and in the mosaic it is the emperor and empress, not the bishop, whose heads are adorned with halos.

Important changes were happening in Rome during this period, too. In the sixth century, the title "pope"—from *papa,* "father"—came to be reserved for the bishop of Rome. This crowned the development of a complex set of ideas about the special status, powers, and prerogatives of the popes, the most important of which was the claim of primacy, or rulership, over the entire Christian church. This claim was based on the pope's spiritual descent from Saint Peter, who was the first bishop of Rome, and it was supported with Jesus's words in the Gospel of Matthew (16:18–19): "You are Peter, the rock, and on this rock I will build my church, and the powers of death shall never conquer it. I will give you the keys of the kingdom of heaven; what you forbid on earth shall be forbidden in heaven, and what you allow on earth shall be allowed in heaven." Peter was first among the apostles, making his diocese, or see, of Rome *the* apostolic see.

Rome's history as the seat of the emperors was also enlisted in support of the idea of papal primacy. Constantine, the first emperor to convert to Christianity, supposedly donated to Pope Sylvester I (314–

335) not only primacy over all other churches, but also imperial power over the city of Rome, Italy, and "all western regions," in addition to the ceremonial honors usually reserved for emperors. This "Donation of Constantine" was proven to be a pious forgery in the fifteenth century, but in the Middle Ages it was believed to be valid. During this period, popes were claiming equality with, if not superiority to, emperors.[6] Writing to Emperor Anastasius in 494, Pope Gelasius I asserted the following:

> There are two things, of course, venerable emperor, by which this world is chiefly ruled: the sacred authority of priests [*sacerdotium*] and the royal power [*regnum*]. Of these, the burden of priests is weightier since they will render account at the last judgment even for the souls of kings themselves. In fact you know, most merciful son, that although by your office you rule over the entire human race, you nevertheless faithfully bow the neck to those who have charge of things divine and you seek from them the means of your salvation.[7]

This "Gelasian doctrine" was also called the doctrine of the "two swords"—from the two types of rulership, priestly and royal—and it was highly influential.

The Carolingian Order

The concepts of papal primacy and sacred rulership influenced the new peoples who were moving into the West between the third and sixth centuries. It took a long time to Christianize these Germanic peoples, but their conversion was achieved gradually, often through missionaries sent from Rome. The Germanic peoples had their own indigenous concept of priest-kings and ultimately accommodated and transformed the potent model of sacred rulership created by the merger of late Roman political culture and Christianity. By the ninth century, a new amalgam of traditions had produced a model of European kingship that not only fused the concepts of power and the holy, but made the western church an active partner in the making of monarchs.

The key innovators here were the Carolingians, a dynasty that came to rule the Franks, a Germanic people, in the mid-eighth century. The Franks had settled in the heart of Europe, roughly in what is today the nation of France. In 751, an enterprising chief administrator named Pippin gained papal approval to depose the last Merovingian monarch and become the first Carolingian king of the Franks. He legitimized this coup by skillfully manipulating religious support and symbolism. He gave military protection to the pope when Rome was threatened by the advance of another Germanic people, the Lombards. Pippin facilitated the work of missionaries in his kingdom, and key bishops supported him. In 754 Pope Stephen II traveled all the way from Rome to bless King Pippin and to anoint his head—and those of his sons Charles and Carloman—with holy oil. Peasants who glimpsed this could relate it to the baptismal rite in which a new Christian, washed clean of sin, was anointed; more literate viewers might recall how Samuel in the Old Testament (1 Sam. 16:13) used oil to anoint King David so that "the spirit of the Lord came upon David and was with him from that day onwards."

This close relationship between the papacy and the Carolingians transformed Europe under the rule of Pippin's son, the young Charles whom Pope Stephen II had anointed. Better known to history as Charlemagne or Charles the Great (768–814), this dynamic king conquered much of what we today call Europe, turning the Frankish kingdom into an empire. On Christmas Day in 800, Charles received the title his conquests implied: Pope Leo III crowned him emperor. He was hailed as a "new Constantine," "Charles Augustus, crowned by God." But what those in Saint Peter's basilica saw, and what others heard later, was that the *pope* had crowned Charlemagne, making him emperor. This set an important precedent for later, more powerful, popes. Charlemagne, like his father, had come to Rome to protect the pope from his enemies. Charlemagne's service to the church, however, went well beyond defending the papacy. He gave generously to monasteries, making them dynamic centers of teaching and learning, as well as bringing new rigor and standardization to their way of life through wide dissemination of the Rule of Saint Benedict, a guide to the monastic life written just outside of Rome in the sixth century by Saint Benedict of Nursia. The emperor also expanded efforts that his father had begun to reform the church, setting important precedents and traditions. He called councils that legislated against abuses. This disseminated a Constantinian model of royal oversight of the church in western Europe and furthered the development of ecclesiastical (or "canon") law. Charlemagne worked with bishops closely in these reforming efforts and depended upon them heavily in the administration of his realm. He appointed bishops and organized his conquests into ecclesiastical provinces.

The Carolingians disseminated throughout Europe a concept of church reform that sought to restore pristine Christian practice by looking to Rome. Pippin and Charlemagne, for example, tried to standardize the ecclesiastical liturgies or ceremonies celebrated throughout their dominions by getting copies of manuscripts from Rome and importing Roman clerics to teach priests the chants and prayers of the Roman liturgy.[8] To medieval people, reform meant restoring ancient traditions, not innovating or seeking new solutions. For Europeans after the ninth century these venerable Christian customs derived from Rome.

The Carolingian Crisis

The elaboration of this new Carolingian order, however, was cut short. Charlemagne's grandsons divided his empire, and then new waves of invasions crippled their power. From the east, the Hungarians conducted annual raids into the German duchies and the plains of northern Italy from 899. From the south, Muslim bands attacked the coasts of France and Italy. The most feared marauders, however, came from the north. The Vikings, or "northmen," plundered communities throughout northern Europe during the ninth and tenth centuries, conquering England and Ireland. They ran highly lucrative extortion rackets in northern Francia, and one of the later Carolingians, Charles the Simple, ceded part of his kingdom to them. This was later called "Normandy" after the "northmen" who had made it theirs. The cession of territory to Viking leaders reveals the weakness of kings in the face of such swift and unpredictable raids, especially in the western portions of the old Carolingian empire. In the east, in the German duchies, a new dynasty—the Ottonians—emerged to defend against the invaders. Its success was rewarded in 962 when Pope John XII granted the imperial title to Otto I. This transfer of the imperial crown from the rulers of Francia to the kings of the nascent German empire forged a powerful bond between the papacy and Otto's successors.

The new powers that emerged as the Carolingian order crumbled, however, were generally not as lofty as the Ottonians. Particularly in Francia, when royal power did not adequately protect communities, new local leaders emerged to offer some defense. They built fortifications and organized their own private armies. Towns, villages, monasteries, and other ecclesiastical institutions paid these new local potentates for protection, ceding lands and treasure to them. Over the tenth and eleventh centuries, these local strongmen formed a newly powerful nobility. When the outside invasions ceased, they waged war on one another to secure dominance of larger territories, and they terrorized their own populations to exact more revenues. The church and the peasantry bore the brutal brunt of this transfer of power—and they allied to curb it.

MOVEMENTS FOR REFORM

Bishops had been accustomed to wielding power in the Carolingian empire, and from the late tenth century they positioned themselves as saviors of the people. They called together local populations in "peace councils" and organized "truces of God" to try to limit violence (Documents 1 and 2). Although not tremendously effective, their efforts encouraged people such as peasants, merchants, and clerics to look to ecclesiastical leaders to limit the power of unjust rulers. In the peace councils, bishops summoned local lords to their presence and convinced many of them to take oaths to abandon certain violent exactions and practices. They were able to do so by virtue of their spiritual authority: They could threaten miscreant nobles with exclusion from the sacraments of the church, which was equivalent to a sentence of eternal damnation. The bishops not only used their own sacred powers, but they called in the saints to help them. By bringing the relics (i.e., bodily remains) of the saints to these gatherings and having peace oaths taken upon them, these ecclesiastical leaders suggested that holy objects and miraculous powers were more important in bringing order to society than the actions of local lords or kings. Such associations encouraged people to look to ecclesiastical leaders for justice and to believe that holy protectors were necessary for peace and order.[9]

While the social prestige (or "cultural capital") of the holy was increasing, the actual condition of ecclesiastical institutions and the character of their ministers appeared to be declining. The invasions had adversely affected them. Through cessions or conquests of property, many churches had come under the control of proprietors who were not terribly concerned about the spiritual needs of their congregations. The clergy that their power permitted them to appoint to these churches were often not of the highest quality. Unrest had disrupted what few schools and clerical communities trained priests, so there may not have been enough qualified candidates to be appointed.

And rising hopes for divine succor may have influenced contemporary expectations of the clergy. Whatever the causes, many people were dissatisfied with their parish priests. A popular preacher in Milan (Document 6) complained that priests "openly take wives just like laymen, pursue debauchery just like the most wicked laymen," and live luxuriously off the donations of the faithful.

Monastic communities were also hurt by disorder. Targeted by the invaders because of their gold and silver liturgical vessels and reliquaries, monasteries were repeatedly sacked. Many communities had to flee their monasteries in search of security, and such travails impeded the regular routine of prayer that was the foundation of monastic life. This disruption was disconcerting not only for monks; it upset lay elites as well. This was due to the specialized division of labor in the early medieval economy of salvation: Monks prayed, and people paid these experts to offer prayers on their own and their relatives' behalf. If the quality of monastic life and prayer declined, the souls of the deceased relatives of monastic benefactors would be imperiled. Thus, the first efforts at ameliorating the effects of disorder and reforming ecclesiastical institutions were aimed at monasteries.

Chronological priority is not, however, the only reason to begin our consideration of reform with monasticism, for changes in monastic life underscore the diversity and local impetus that drove reform in the eleventh century. Whereas earlier Carolingian attempts at reform had been organized by the royal court and radiated outward, Europe no longer enjoyed the unity of Charlemagne's empire. Thus, reform in the eleventh century was a "grass-roots" effort. Individuals and communities pursued their own visions of reform, and while some broad tendencies and common themes emerge across the eleventh century, there was no one, unified reform movement. Instead, there were many local movements throughout Europe.

The renewal of religious life began independently at many different monasteries. Pious nobles like Duke William of Aquitaine endowed new monasteries dedicated to a rigorous life of prayer in accordance with the Benedictine Rule. The house William founded in 910 at Cluny in Burgundy (Document 3) was quite successful, but so too were foundations to the north in Lotharingia and further south in Italy. Monasteries near one another often formed reform "circles," and there were contacts and influences among these various networks, but for the most part they developed independently. Reform was also accomplished in many different ways: Bishops, kings, and lay elites fostered reform, but those of more modest backgrounds also contributed.

Charismatic hermits, like Saint Romuald of Ravenna (Document 4) and Robert of Arbrissel (Document 31), inspired many to take up the monastic life and reform monasteries or found new ones. Romuald had given up significant family wealth to become a hermit, but Robert was a peasant from a small village in Brittany.[10]

It must be noted at this point that the papacy was a latecomer to reform. Noble families within the city of Rome had long competed to control the power and wealth of the see of Saint Peter. They were a contributing factor to Leo III's difficulties in Charlemagne's time, and their intrigue increased as Carolingian power waned. It was only through the intervention of Emperor Henry III at the Synod of Sutri in 1046 (Document 13) and through the nomination of his kinsman, Bruno of Toul, as pope in 1048 (Document 14) that the papacy was wrested from the control of Roman clans and became a force for reform. It remained, however, only one center of reform among many: Monasteries, individual bishops, and rulers like Henry III were all working for reform. Although most Europeans could agree on the goals of reform, their ideas about the means necessary to accomplish them varied widely. Even those most closely associated with the papacy differed vociferously on key issues. Just one example is provided by the different views on simony (Documents 9 and 10) propounded by two monks: Humbert of Silva Candida (ca. 1006–1061), who was made a cardinal by Pope Leo IX in 1051, and Peter Damian (1007–1072), a hermit of Fonte Avellana in the rugged mountains of central Italy, who often served as a legate, or emissary, of the reformed papacy.

There was greater unanimity on the problems plaguing the church than on the solutions to them. Three issues recur across the eleventh century in sources from all over Europe: clerical celibacy, simony, and "canonical" or "free" election.

Clerical celibacy seemed the easiest to define but was the most difficult to enforce. Many laypeople seemed to want their priests to be pure so that the sacraments those priests offered to them would effectively transmit the grace that was believed to be necessary for salvation. Sexual activity was perceived to be a source of impurity and therefore a threat to the efficacy of the sacraments. Although there were ancient church laws forbidding priests to marry or have concubines, over the early Middle Ages these restrictions had, in practice, been abandoned. Economic factors played a role. Churches were usually endowed with lands to support the priest, but those lands had to be worked and a household maintained in order to produce the food and clothing a priest needed to survive. Since the family was the standard productive unit of the medieval economy, many priests created families. Surely many also enjoyed the companionship and affection of family ties. For ecclesiastical leaders, however, the wives and children of priests posed a threat to church property. Fathers usually bequeath property to their children (Document 36), and communities are often reluctant to turn widows and children out of their homes. These very human and humane impulses allowed church properties to slip into private hands. Many ecclesiastical leaders and laypeople perceived clerical marriage and concubinage as a serious problem with no easy solution. Bishops were well aware that if they got rid of all their married clergy, few would be left to provide adequate pastoral care. Should priests simply abandon their wives? Some reacted violently to what they perceived as a novel requirement: The clergy of Rouen pelted their archbishop with stones when he demanded that they give up their women.[11]

Simony, the buying and selling of anything considered spiritual, was declared an evil custom, even a heresy. If a priest charged a sum of money to perform a baptism, the act was clearly simony. But what if the joyful parents gave the priest a gift after the ceremony as a token of their appreciation? Was that simony? Or if the priest were promised some benefit (a future exchange of lands or a promotion to a better church) for baptizing the child? Most problematic were promotions to offices, especially ones like bishoprics that were rich in lands and rights. Kings and emperors were accused of selling bishoprics to the highest bidder. Over the course of the eleventh century, as those promoting reform debated these issues, clearer definitions of what constituted simony were developed.[12] The implications of simony, however, were vastly more difficult to confront. If a bishop gained his office through simony, did that mean he wasn't really a bishop and therefore none of the men he had ordained were really priests? And what about the sacraments those priests had administered? If your parish priest had been ordained by a simoniacal bishop, did that mean your children weren't really baptized and were, therefore, in danger of burning in eternal hellfire after death? Reformers were forced to deal with these vexing questions (Documents 9 and 10).

The custom of powerful laypeople appointing ecclesiastical officials also created dissent. Although early church law had set out that important officials such as bishops should be elected "by clergy and people," kings and local lords had become accustomed to choosing men for these positions. The roles of both the clergy and laypeople were effectively reduced to only giving their consent by acclamation to a candidate chosen by a ruler (Document 11). Many kings and nobles piously believed that it was their duty to help provide for the spiritual welfare of their subjects and so considered it their responsibility to find and appoint the best bishop possible. Others, however, simply saw an opportunity to appoint a relative or friend to an office with rich estates and lucrative rights. The custom was also fostered by a strong sense of property rights: If there's a church on your property, why shouldn't you be able to decide who officiates in it?[13] Concern on the part of reformers about salvation and the quality of the men serving in churches led to calls to return to "canonical" or "free" election, that ancient custom of election by clergy and people. But the meaning of this was unclear in the eleventh century, since no ancient document spelled out a procedure. Which clergy? Which people? And because kings and lords are part of "the people," shouldn't they have a voice in the election? And what if the clergy and people can't agree on a candidate?

THE INVESTITURE CONFLICT

Everyone recognized that power over ecclesiastical appointments meant power over the church. Thus, the "canonical," or "free," election of church leaders was believed to be essential to the "freedom of the church." It was believed that the church must be free so it could effectively pursue its mission of bringing all souls to salvation. How bishops were made, therefore, was a central reform issue and one reason why contention over reform turned to violent conflict over investiture.

Personalities and human relationships also played a big role. At the center of the investiture conflict were two very complicated human beings: Emperor Henry IV and Pope Gregory VII. Often when two people become fixated on a disagreement over a particular issue, understanding the personal dynamics of their relationship is essential to understanding the conflict. Herein lies the historical fascination of the investiture struggle. Henry and Gregory had a very volatile relationship, and each had a lot going on in his life.

Great expectations surrounded Henry from the moment of his birth on November 11, 1050. His father, the great emperor Henry III, already had four daughters; he needed a son and an heir. Immediately after the young prince's birth, his father set about securing the kingdom for him, calling on the princes of the realm to swear loyalty to the infant. When he was three years old, Henry was formally elected king by an assembly of nobles. Months later he was anointed, crowned, and enthroned in the imperial chapel at Aachen that Charlemagne had built. The hymns sung at the occasion would have greeted Henry as the "vicar of the Creator," "the image of God," the king appointed by God "to rule the whole world."[14] Henry's entire upbringing inculcated a sense of awesome responsibility and a belief in his sacred destiny and royal prerogatives.

When his father died suddenly in 1056, the very young king ascended to the throne under the regency of his mother, Agnes, while factions fought for control over the child monarch. At age twelve, Henry was kidnapped by one of these factions, led by Archbishop Anno of Cologne, who took over the regency. By the time Henry began to rule on his own at age fifteen, he was eager to assert his will and restore both the authority and the wealth of the crown. Henry's efforts began in Saxony and prompted scattered unrest that turned into a major rebellion by the time he reached his early twenties. The rebels held estates and castles, particularly the royal palace at Goslar, that had been favored stops on the royal itinerary. As unrest continued to dog the young king, he became more dependent on the hospitality and resources of the ecclesiastical princes he had appointed. He had, of course, been investing bishops since he was a child. Would he even consider surrendering that prerogative as an adult in the midst of a civil war?

The man who demanded he do so was, like Henry, acting out of a sense of sacred duty and princely prerogative. Pope Gregory VII's name before he ascended to the throne of Saint Peter was Hildebrand, and it was under this name that he came to be known at the court of Henry's father. Hildebrand had been educated at Rome in the papal Lateran palace, and some claim he lived as a monk for a time before entering clerical orders.[15] He had a deep devotion to the Roman church and to the apostles Saints Peter and Paul who were its special patrons. Hildebrand came to the German Empire as a chaplain in the entourage of Pope Gregory VI, one of the three popes Henry III had deposed at the Synod of Sutri in 1046 (Document 13). He returned to Rome three years later in the company of Leo IX, whom the emperor had just appointed pope (Document 14). Hildebrand returned several times to Henry III's realm on papal business, and it seems likely that he was present at the child-king's coronation at Aachen.

Probably about the age of Henry's father, Hildebrand later tended to relate to the king in a paternal fashion, admonishing him frequently about his behavior and addressing him as "son." This age difference and Hildebrand's respect for Henry's father certainly influenced the relationship. By the time he was acclaimed pope on April 22, 1073, by an enthusiastic Roman crowd, Hildebrand had decades of experience in papal ministry. During his years of service to several popes, he had worked avidly for reform and had seen Rome assume a new position of leadership in the campaign to secure the "freedom of the church." As Pope Gregory VII he joined that battle with a ferocious sense of the church's mission in the world. He took his role as the heir of the apostle Peter, whom Christ had chosen as the foundation of his church, just as seriously as Henry IV took his own inheritance to rule as "vicar of Christ."

For both Gregory and Henry, the investiture of bishops took on tremendous significance. The practice came to stand for fundamentally important issues. To Gregory, lay investiture meant that monarchs would continue to appoint as bishops their own creatures—men who thus would not undertake the hard work of reform in their dioceses—imperiling the souls of thousands of Christians. He believed that bishops were representatives of the church and should pursue the Lord's work—as defined by the pope—rather than the king's service. For Gregory and many other reformers, the idea of laymen handing over the sacred objects symbolizing the bishop's authority was sacrilegious, a profanation of holy things. To Henry, investiture was his God-given right, a right exercised by all his forebears and essential to the good order of the realm. The idea that vast estates and powers within his kingdom should be held by men whose loyalty he could not depend on was entirely unacceptable. Moreover, for the pope to interfere in the running of his kingdom seemed an insufferable affront to his royal authority.

Even more disturbing to many contemporaries were Pope Gregory VII's repeated appeals to social inferiors to rise up against their superiors. Hierarchy was considered natural in the Middle Ages; it was part of a divinely ordained world order. "The just God differentiated the life of men," wrote Bishop Ratherius of Verona, "making some slaves and some lords." This tenth-century bishop wrote a long treatise that set out the various ranks in society, from beggars to kings, admonishing each on what was appropriate to their station.[16] Yet, Gregory urged the people of Piacenza to expel their bishop, countenanced parishioners boycotting their priests in Milan, and counseled a lay noblewoman to reject the advice of a priest and high-ranking ecclesiastical dignitary (Document 8).[17] The pope's alliance with vassals who were rebelling against Henry IV struck many nobles as a scandalous upending of right order: "It is novel, and was unknown in any past age," objected Wenrich of Trier, "for priests so easily to bring nations into civil strife, by a sudden act to shatter the name of king, which was discovered at the creation of the world and established by God, contemptuously to dismiss the Lord's anointed as if they were mere bailiffs. . . ."[18]

Gregory certainly exploited Henry's political difficulties. The Saxon princes revolted in 1073 after Henry attempted to reclaim estates in the region once held by his predecessors. The king lost the opening round and was forced to agree to a humiliating peace in February 1074 when the south and central German princes, who sympathized with some of the Saxon grievances, refused to come to his aid. These nobles, however, renewed their support for Henry after a mob of Saxon peasants destroyed the royal palace at Harzburg in March 1074, shockingly desecrating two royal tombs. That summer, Henry won a resounding military victory over the rebels at Homburg, and his investiture of several bishops in the wake of this victory contributed to his first confrontation with Pope Gregory (Document 20).

In February 1076, the pope excommunicated Henry, declared him deposed, and released all his subjects and vassals from their sworn allegiance. By summer, Saxony was again in open revolt, and Gregory was communicating with the German princes about the election of a new king. Although Henry's daring interception of the pope at Canossa resulted in his absolution from the excommunication (Documents 22 and 23), his opposition proceeded to elect an antiking, Rudolf of Swabia, in March 1077, and the civil war consumed Henry's energies. Early in 1080, the pope renewed his excommunication and deposition of Henry, who responded by gathering his bishops at Brixen to condemn Gregory and elect a new pope (Wibert of Ravenna, who took the name Clement III). Within months, events turned in Henry's favor. In October, a messy battle near the Elster river claimed his rival's life. Rudolf of Swabia probably died of a wound in his side, but another wound was considered more significant by contemporaries: The antiking had lost his right hand in the battle. This was deemed an appropriate punishment for having broken his oath of fealty to his king, and thus Henry's victory was seen as a divine judgment. As Henry's anonymous biographer concluded, the manner of Rudolf's death was "a great lesson to the world that no one may rebel against his lord."[19]

With this sense of divine vindication, Henry IV marched on Rome in 1081. It took years of diplomacy and siege warfare, but finally in

Map 1. Key Cities and Monasteries in the Investiture Conflict, ca. 1075–1122.

Map 2. Important European Regions during the Investiture Conflict, ca. 1075–1122.

21

March 1084 Henry took Saint Peter's basilica. A number of cardinals who had defected from Gregory consecrated Henry's candidate, Wibert of Ravenna, as Pope Clement III and enthroned him. Clement then crowned Henry emperor. Meanwhile, Gregory, who had retreated to the fortress of Castel Sant'Angelo on the banks of the Tiber, called in his Norman allies from southern Italy. Henry and Clement III withdrew from Rome to avoid confronting the much larger Norman force, but the Norman army's destruction of many Roman neighborhoods turned the population against Gregory. The pope was forced to retreat to Salerno, where he died May 25, 1085 (Document 28). Gregory's successors, however, continued the struggle. Pope Urban II drove Clement III out of Rome in 1089, and in 1093 he supported the rebellion of Henry's son, Conrad. In 1105, another of Henry's sons, Henry V, seized power and forced his aged father to abdicate. Henry IV died seven months later on August 7, 1106.

The bitter conflict between Gregory and Henry over investiture consumed their lives and continued after their deaths. A series of compromises, spelled out in the agreements at Worms in 1122 (Document 30), brought an official end to the struggle. But many issues remained unresolved, and the implications and consequences of reform were still being realized over the twelfth and thirteenth centuries.

THE CONSEQUENCES OF REFORM

The results of the reform movements and the investiture conflict went far beyond the original goals of those demanding change. There were some unintended consequences that were part of the broad transformations that unfolded across the twelfth and thirteenth centuries.

Lay Engagement with the Faith

Reform profoundly altered the status and experience of laypeople within the church. While members of the clergy had always held a more exalted status than laypeople because of their power over all things sacred, the tendency in the early Middle Ages was for most clerics to live and act much like laypeople, which blurred distinctions between the groups. Reform not only reinscribed the status distinctions, but deepened them. This was mainly due to a new emphasis on, and exaltation of, the powers of the priesthood. In the course of arguing for changes in clerical behavior, advocates of reform more carefully defined and highlighted the special role of priests in transmitting the grace necessary for salvation through the sacraments. Calls for the "freedom of the church" from lay interference also fostered a tendency to identify the church with the clergy, which ran counter to an older tradition that conceived of the church as the entire community of the faithful—clergy and laity.[20]

At the same time, the rising spiritual aspirations of laypeople challenged attempts to distinguish lay from clerical roles and to subordinate the laity to clerical authority. The notion of what it meant to live a religious life was changing. In the early Middle Ages, it meant abandoning the world to lead a monastic life of prayer and contemplation under the Rule of Saint Benedict. Over the eleventh century, however, a life in the world, patterned on the actions of Jesus and his disciples, gained broader acceptance as a kind of religious life. This "apostolic life," or *vita apostolica,* was emphasized as a charismatic model for the clergy, who—like Christ and the apostles—lived in the world, ministering to the people through preaching and teaching. Clerics were exhorted to embrace the communal life of Jesus and his disciples, as well as the celibacy he and the apostles cultivated. Once the concept of leading a life of holiness in the world was introduced, many laypeople rushed to embrace it.

Across the twelfth century, informal groups of pious laypeople formed with the goal of living an "apostolic life" (Documents 32 and 33). The clergy enthusiastically supported lay initiatives to feed the poor, care for the sick, and gather for prayer. But when laypeople wanted to preach, ecclesiastical leaders grew nervous, and concerns about heresy increased. Preaching had been a means of spreading ideas about reform and cultivating lay support for it. Indeed, many people had been inspired by the ideal of the "apostolic life" through the words of charismatic preachers (Document 31). While sermons became an important focus of lay devotion in the wake of the movements for reform, control of preaching became a persistent struggle between the clergy and the laity. Many lay groups, such as the Waldensians (Document 32), were condemned as heretical because they refused to obey clerical orders to stop preaching.[21]

The inspiration of the apostolic life also enlivened interest in the places where Jesus of Nazareth had lived. If being a good Christian meant, as many increasingly believed, patterning one's life after Christ's, then pilgrimage to the Holy Land allowed the believer to walk in the footsteps of the Savior. Such pious journeys seemed to increase during the eleventh century. Thus, at the Council of Clermont in 1095, when Pope Urban II urged western Christians to liberate the Holy Land from the infidels who had desecrated those holy places (Document 34), he tapped into a rich devotional current that he used to channel objectionable lay energies into the service of the church.[22] Since the "peace councils" of the late tenth and early eleventh centuries, ecclesiastical leaders had seen a connection between the endemic violence of the knightly classes and the problems plaguing the church. In addition to trying to limit violence, the peace councils had legislated against seizures of ecclesiastical lands, payments demanded for the sacraments, and clerics bearing arms (Document 2). Reform was also the motive of the Council of Clermont, which promulgated decrees against simony and lay control of churches.

The Council of Clermont's call for an "armed pilgrimage" or "crusade" to the Holy Land, moreover, articulated an ingenious solution to the problem of elite violence within western Europe. The pope urged those waging wars within Europe to turn their arms against the infidels and liberate the Holy Sepulcher in Jerusalem. Remission of sins would be their reward. The wildly popular movement that Urban's sermon launched fostered the pacification of Europe in two ways. First, it exported some of the most violent and unruly elements in western society, directing their aggression outward. Second, the church's offer of spiritual merit for participation in military campaigns began the Christianization of knighthood.[23] The attempt to change knightly behavior and provide a code of Christian ethics for knighthood was an important elaboration of reform goals (Document 35).

The Unfolding of Reform within the Church

Clerical life and institutions also changed as a result of the reform movements and the investiture conflict. Although many of the problems reformers addressed resisted tidy solutions, key concepts—that priests should be celibate and that spiritual things could not be sold—gained acceptance, and a new decorum was established (Document 36). Although the behavior of the clergy continued to elicit criticism (Document 37), the standards applied to their behavior were no longer contested. Of the three original burning issues of the reform movements, "canonical" or "free" election was least successfully resolved. Monarchs continued to be involved in the making of bishops, and conflicts multiplied (Documents 38 and 39). By the beginning of the thirteenth century, disputed elections had resulted in so many cases being appealed to the papal court that popes simply began appointing or "providing" bishops to their sees. Papal provision progressively replaced election "by clergy and people."

The most important consequence of the investiture conflict for the church was the enormous increase in the power of the papacy. Gregory VII had claimed extraordinary powers as pope, but he was neither theoretically nor practically successful in winning recognition for those claims. Gregory's successors, however, transformed his expansive vision of the papacy into a reality. They did so by developing compelling theological and legal foundations for papal authority, by building powerful and efficient institutions to enforce papal mandates (Document 40), and by cultivating the ceremony and splendor that people expected in rulers (Document 41). In sum, "papal monarchy," which was realized over the twelfth century, was one of the most significant results of the reform movements and the investiture conflict.[24] But it was accomplished at a price. Papal interference in local ecclesiastical matters bred resentment, and the splendor cultivated by the papal court provoked criticism (Document 43). Both of these objections to papal monarchy were, centuries later, powerful factors contributing to the Protestant Reformation.

Sanctity and Just Rulership

The most radical innovation of the papal reformers was their challenge to the sacred character of kings. Implicit in the concept of "lay investiture" was the idea that kings were laymen. Yet kings were anointed, and in the eleventh century most people, including ecclesiastics, viewed royal consecration as akin to priestly ordination. It was a sacrament that made the king "a new man." Many regarded the anointing of monarchs as conferring clerical status, and kings usually were numbered among the canons in various cathedral chapters. Emperors after their coronation became canons of St. Peter's in Rome.[25]

Only the most radical reformers challenged this belief in the sanctity of monarchs. The earliest evidence comes in the *Three Books against the Simoniacs,* where Humbert of Silva Candida ignores the sacred status of kings altogether and considers them purely as laymen. As laymen, kings may not elect or invest bishops or other ecclesiastical officials, Humbert argues. Gregory VII's position was more complicated and usually avoided direct comment on the status of kings. But he clearly considered the royal "dignity" to be contingent upon appropriate kingly behavior: Only through obedience to the Holy See and proper humility could the royal power guide human society in concord with the priestly power. And Gregory definitely saw the priestly dignity as far superior to the royal office. Most telling is his explicit ranking of kings below the minor clerical order of exorcist (Document 26).[26] This placement of royal dignity is especially significant in the context of late-eleventh-century Rome, where, as a result of the reformers' exaltation of the priesthood, those in the minor clerical orders were being demoted to "semi-lay" status.[27]

Although pro-papal theorists utilized these desacralized notions of rulership to argue for significant limitations on royal power, most Europeans continued to believe that kings were sacred personages. Moreover, one of the most significant results of the investiture conflict was that monarchs, with the help of their supporters, intensified their claims to holiness. New powers of healing were attributed to kings in the twelfth century (Document 45), and monarchs actively propagated the cults of royal saints (Document 46). In symbols, ritual, architecture, and funerary practices, kings more aggressively asserted their sacred character (Documents 47 and 48).[28] Although it is significant, therefore, that a concept of secular rulership was articulated during the investiture conflict, it is just as important to recognize that it was not accepted. Power and the holy were *more* complexly and inextricably intertwined as a result of the struggle over reform.

THE CONTEMPORARY LEGACY

What the investiture conflict and its aftermath accomplished was to place the relationship between power and the holy at the forefront of thought and debate. In this sense, we are still working out the heritage of these historical events. In the late eleventh century, questions concerning the nature of power and holiness and the proper relationship between the two provoked enormous controversy. Such questions have been the subject of political debate ever since, and they still regularly inflame public opinion. In contemporary U.S. political discourse, controversies over power and the holy most frequently concern objects and space (copies of the Ten Commandments displayed in public buildings, or menorahs and Nativity scenes decorating parks). Medieval people were also vitally concerned about sacred objects — the bishop's staff and ring being central to the investiture controversy — but they were more focused on sacred persons and their claims to authority.

When and why did people stop wanting their rulers to be holy? Divine-right monarchs were overthrown in seventeenth- and eighteenth-century Europe, and governmental systems based on the popular will were established. But were power and the holy divorced, or did the holy just migrate? Are "the people" themselves seen as sacred in the modern era? Or if not the people themselves, is their "will" or expressions of it, such as the U.S. Constitution (which is often called a "sacred" document), sacred? How is holiness invoked in contemporary political discourse? The sonorous rhetoric of Pope Gregory VII and Emperor Henry IV about the "right order" of the world differs in style and substance from our own political speech, but some of the issues raised by their eloquent conflict are still with us today.

NOTES

[1]Andrew of Strumi, *Vita sancti Arialdi,* ed. F. Baethgen. In *Monumenta Germaniae Historica Scriptores,* vol. 30, part 2 (Leipzig: Hiersemann, 1934), 1057.

[2]I. S. Robinson, *Authority and Resistance in the Investiture Contest: The Polemical Literature of the Late Eleventh Century* (Manchester and New York: Manchester University Press/Holmes & Meier, 1978); Augustin Fliche, *La réforme grégorienne,* 3 vols., Spicilegium sacrum Lovaniensis, Études et documents 6, 9, 16 (Louvain: Spicilegium sacrum Lovaniensis, and Paris: E. Champion, 1924–1937); Gerd Tellenbach, *Church, State and Christian Society at the Time of the Investiture Contest,* trans. R. F. Bennett (Toronto: University of Toronto Press / Mediaeval Academy of America, 1991); an overview in English of the historiography may be found in the introduction to Norman F. Cantor, *Church, Kingship and Lay Investiture in England, 1089–1135* (Princeton: Princeton University Press, 1958; rpt. New York: Octagon Books, 1969).

[3]André Vauchez, *The Laity in the Middle Ages: Religious Beliefs and Devotional Practices,* trans. Margery J. Schneider (Notre Dame: University of Notre Dame Press, 1993), 41.

[4]Gerd Tellenbach, *The Church in Western Europe from the Tenth to the Early Twelfth Century,* trans. Timothy Reuter (Cambridge, U.K.: Cambridge University Press, 1993), 39–42.

[5]Clifford Ando, *Imperial Ideology and Provincial Loyalty in the Roman Empire* (Berkeley and Los Angeles: University of California Press, 2000), esp. xi–xiii, 206–73; Richard Gordon, "From Republic and Principate: Priesthood, Religion and Ideology," and "The Veil of Power: Emperors, Sacrificers and Benefactors." In *Pagan Priests: Religion and Power in the Ancient World,* ed. Mary Beard and John North (Ithaca, N.Y.: Cornell University Press, 1990), 177–231.

[6]Bernhard Schimmelpfennig, *The Papacy,* trans. James Sievert (New York: Columbia University Press, 1992), 15–46.

[7]*Publizistische Sammlungen zum Acacianischen Schisma,* ed. E. Schwartz. Abhandlungen der Bayerischen Akademie der Wissenschaften, Philosophische-Historische Abteilung, Neue Folge 10 (Munich, 1934), 20.

[8]Pierre Riché, *The Carolingians: A Family Who Forged Europe,* trans. Michael Idomir Allen (Philadelphia: University of Pennsylvania Press, 1993), 66–72, 76–77, 117–23, 146.

[9]*The Peace of God: Social Violence and Religious Response in France around the Year 1000,* ed. Thomas Head and Richard Landes (Ithaca, N.Y.: Cornell University Press, 1992).

[10]Kassius Hallinger, *Gorze-Kluny: Studien zu den monastischen Lebensformen und Gegensätzen im Hochmittelalter,* 2 vols. (Graz: Akadem. Druck-u. Verlagsanst., 1971); Uta-Renate Blumenthal, *The Investiture Controversy: Church and Monarchy from the Ninth to the Twelfth Century* (Philadelphia: University of Pennsylvania Press, 1988), 7–22; Grado Giovanni Merlo, "Le riforme monastiche e la 'vita apostolica.'" In *Storia dell'Italia religiosa, 1: L'antichità e il medioevo,* ed. André Vauchez (Rome: Laterza, 1993), 271–91; Milo Yoram, "Dissonance between Papal and Local Reform Interests in Pre-Gregorian Tuscany," *Studi Medievali,* ser. 3, 20 (1979): 69–86; Joachim Wollasch, "Monasticism: The First Wave of Reform." In *The New Cambridge Medieval History, III: c. 900–c. 1024,* ed. Timothy Reuter (Cambridge, U.K.: Cambridge University Press, 1995), 162–85; John Howe, "The Nobility's Reform of the Medieval Church," *American Historical Review,* 93 (1988): 317–39.

[11]Bishop Ratherius of Verona remarked in exasperation, "If I were to expel from the clergy those with many wives, whom would I leave in the church except boys? If I were to cast out the bastards, whom of these boys would I permit in the choir?" *The Complete Works of Rather of Verona,* trans. Peter L. D. Reid (Binghamton, N.Y.: Medieval & Renaissance Texts & Studies, 1991), 472; for the canons of Rouen and other examples of clerical protest against the demand for celibacy, see John E. Lynch, "Marriage and Celibacy of the Clergy—The Discipline of the Western Church: An Historico-Canonical Synopsis," *The Jurist,* 32 (1972): 194.

[12]See John Gilchrist, "'Simoniaca Haeresis' and the Problem of Orders from Leo IX to Gratian," *Proceedings of the Second International Congress of Medieval Canon Law, Boston College, 12–16 August 1963,* ed. Stephan Kuttner and J. Joseph Ryan (Vatican City: S. Congregatio de Seminariis et Studiorum Universitatibus, 1965), 209–35 on the complexities, logical and linguistic, in defining simony.

[13]"Proprietary churches" figure prominently in debates about reform: See Blumenthal, *Investiture Controversy,* 4–7, and bibliography on 24.

[14]I. S. Robinson, *Henry IV of Germany, 1056–1106* (Cambridge, U.K.: Cambridge University Press, 1999), 14; the classic treatment is Ernst H. Kantorowicz, *Laudes Regiae: A Study in Liturgical Acclamations and Mediaeval Ruler Worship* (Berkeley and Los Angeles: University of California Press, 1946).

[15]There is debate on this point: H. E. J. Cowdrey—*Pope Gregory VII, 1073–1085* (Oxford: Clarendon Press, 1998), 28–29—follows late-eleventh-century identifications of Gregory as a monk, but Uta-Renate Blumenthal has pointed out problems with this evidence and suggested that Gregory was trained as a canon: *Gregor VII.: Papst zwischen Canossa und Kirchenreform* (Darmstadt: Primus, 2001), 31–43.

[16]Ratherius was quoting an earlier authority, Isidore of Seville: *The Complete Works of Rather of Verona,* 48.

[17]*The Register of Pope Gregory VII, 1073–1085,* trans. H. E. J. Cowdrey (Oxford: Oxford University Press, 2002), 147 [2.54]; Cowdrey, *Pope Gregory VII,* 280–89.

[18]Tellenbach, *Church, State and Christian Society,* 159–60.

[19]Robinson, *Henry IV,* 204–5; *Imperial Lives and Letters of the Eleventh Century,* trans. Theodor E. Mommsen and Karl F. Morrison (New York: Columbia University Press, 2000), 111.

[20]Vauchez, *The Laity in the Middle Ages,* 41–43. On the new emphasis on the priesthood, see Johannes Laudage, *Priesterbild und Reformpapsttum im 11. Jahrhundert* (Cologne: Böhlau, 1984).

[21]Herbert Grundmann, *Religious Movements in the Middle Ages,* trans. Steven Rowan (Notre Dame and London: University of Notre Dame Press, 1995); R. I. Moore, *The*

Birth of Popular Heresy (London: Edward Arnold, 1975; rpt. Toronto: University of Toronto Press/Medieval Academy of America, 1996) and *The Origins of European Dissent* (New York: St. Martin's, 1977; rpt. Toronto: University of Toronto Press/Medieval Academy of America, 1994).

[22]Paul Alphandéry, *La chrétienté et l'idée de croisade* (Paris: Albin Michel, 1954–9; rpt. 1995), esp. 9–42, 497–513; James A. Brundage, *Medieval Canon Law and the Crusader* (Madison, Milwaukee, and London: University of Wisconsin Press, 1969), 3–18.

[23]Ibid., 19–29; for students, a good introduction to the Christianization of knighthood can be found in Constance Brittain Bouchard, *Strong of Body, Brave & Noble: Chivalry and Society in Medieval France* (Ithaca, N.Y.: Cornell University Press, 1998), 81–85, 122ff; Georges Duby, *The Chivalrous Society,* trans. Cynthia Postan (Berkeley and Los Angeles: University of California Press, 1977), 158–70, also makes these connections succinctly.

[24]Walter Ullmann, *The Growth of Papal Government in the Middle Ages: A Study in the Ideological Relation of Clerical to Lay Power* (London: Bradford & Dickens, 1955; 2nd ed. 1962), esp. 310–43; the ceremonial developments have received the most recent attention: Agostino Paravicini Bagliani, *Le chiavi e la tiara: Immagini e simboli del papato medievale* (Rome: Viella, 1998); Ingo Herklotz, *Gli Eredi di Costantino: Il papato, il Laterano e la propaganda visiva nel XII secolo* (Rome: Viella, 2000); Agostino Paravicini Bagliani, *The Pope's Body,* trans. David S. Peterson (Chicago and London: University of Chicago Press, 2000).

[25]Tellenbach, *Church, State and Christian Society,* 57; Fritz Kern, *Kingship and Law in the Middle Ages,* trans. S. B. Chrimes (Oxford: Basil Blackwell, 1968), 36–40; Sergio Bertelli, *The King's Body: Sacred Rituals of Power in Medieval and Early Modern Europe,* trans. R. Burr Litchfield (University Park: Pennsylvania State University Press, 2001), 14.

[26]Tellenbach, *Church, State and Christian Society,* 108–9; Cowdrey, *Pope Gregory VII,* 608–17.

[27]Tommaso di Carpegna Falconieri, *Il clero di Roma nel medioevo: Istituzioni e politica cittadina (secoli VIII–XIII)* (Rome: Viella, 2002), 136–48.

[28]Marc Bloch, *The Royal Touch: Sacred Monarchy and Scrofula in England and France,* trans. J. E. Anderson (London: Routledge & Kegan Paul, 1973); Bertelli, *The King's Body,* 26–27, 31–34. See also Gábor Kaniczay, *Holy Rulers and Blessed Princesses: Dynastic Cults in Medieval Central Europe,* trans. Éva Pálmai (Cambridge, U.K.: Cambridge University Press, 2002); Robert Folz, *Les saints rois du moyen âge en occident, VIe–XIIIe siècles* (Brussels: Société des Bollandistes, 1984).

PART TWO

The Documents

1

Movements for Reform

The investiture conflict grew out of eleventh-century movements for reform. The concerns these movements raised first appear in various responses to the disorder that accompanied the demise of the Carolingian order in the ninth and tenth centuries and wreaked havoc on communities and ecclesiastical institutions. Two late-tenth-century responses to this disorder, in particular, foreshadow eleventh-century developments: the Peace and Truce of God, and monastic reform. As calls for reform escalated in the eleventh century, three issues emerged most prominently: clerical celibacy, simony, and canonical or "free" election. These issues provoked concern at all levels of European society. The Pataria movement in Milan drew support for its campaign against married and simoniacal clerics from poor urban dwellers, artisans, well-to-do merchants, and members of the nobility. Rulers were also working for reform. Indeed, it was through the efforts of Emperor Henry III of the German Empire that the papacy became a potent force leading and supporting reform efforts.

Responses to the Carolingian Crisis

1

RODULFUS GLABER

Description of the Peace and Truce of God
ca. 1036–1046

Beginning in the late tenth century, ecclesiastical leaders organized gatherings in an attempt to restrain the worst excesses of certain new secular lords and to promote peace. At these councils, the bishops called on local lords to take oaths renouncing certain kinds of violence. These episcopal limitations on violence were called "the Peace of God." Later attempts to restrict times when warfare could be conducted were dubbed "the Truce of God." These accounts were written by Rodulfus Glaber, a monk at Saint-Germain-d'Auxerre (in Francia), probably between ca. 1036 and 1046.

At the millennium of the Lord's Passion [1033], which followed these years of want and disaster, by divine mercy and goodness the violent rainstorms ended. The happy face of the sky began to brighten and to blow with pleasant breezes and by gentle serenity to reveal the magnanimity of the Creator. The entire surface of the earth was graciously flourishing and promised an abundance of produce sufficient to drive away want altogether. It was then that the bishops and abbots and other men of Aquitaine faithful to holy religion first summoned great councils of the whole people, to which the bodies of many saints and innumerable caskets of holy relics were brought. The movement spread from there to the provinces of Arles and Lyons, then throughout Burgundy and into the furthest corners of France. It was decreed through the whole diocese that in fixed places the bishops and magnates of the entire region should convene councils for re-establishing peace and restoring the customs of the holy faith. When the people

Rodulfus Glaber, *Historiarum libri quinque* 4.5.14–17 and 5.1.15, ed. John France (Oxford: Clarendon Press, 1989), 194–98, 236–38.

heard this, the great, middling, and poor came rejoicing, all ready to obey the commands of the pastors of the church no less than if they had been given by a voice from heaven speaking to men on earth. For they were still terrified by all the disasters of the recent past, and feared that they might not attain future abundance and plenty.

A list divided into chapters was drawn up containing both all that was prohibited and all that they had determined, by a solemn vow, to offer to Almighty God. The most important of these was that the peace should be preserved inviolate so that both lay and religious men, whatever dangers had threatened them before, could now go about their business without fear and unarmed. For the robber and the man who seized another's property, having been stopped by the severity of the law, were to suffer either a heavy fine or harsh corporal punishment. Nevertheless, the holy places of all churches were to be held in such honor and reverence that if someone guilty of any crime fled there he would escape unharmed, unless he had violated the aforementioned peace oath, in which case he could be seized before the altar and would suffer the prescribed penalty. Similarly, all clerics, monks, and nuns were to be held in such reverence that those traveling with them were not to be harmed by anyone.

Many things were decided at these councils which we think merit reporting. One matter worth recalling is that all agreed, by a perpetual edict, that everyone should abstain from wine on the sixth day of the week, and from meat on the seventh, unless prevented by a grave illness or by an important solemnity. If any circumstance forced some to relax this prohibition a bit, then they were to feed three poor men. Countless sick people were cured at these gatherings of holy men. Lest this seem a paltry matter, know that in many instances as bent arms and legs were returned to their original healthy state, skin was broken, flesh was torn, and blood gushed forth. These things especially offered proof for others prone to doubt. Such enthusiasm was generated that the bishops raised their croziers to the heavens and with their hands extended all cried out with one voice to God: 'Peace! Peace! Peace!' This was the sign of the perpetual covenant of peace they had sworn with God. It was understood that after five years all should repeat this extraordinary gathering in order to confirm the peace. In that same year there was such a great abundance of corn and wine and other foods that the like could not be hoped to be equaled in the following five years. All food was cheap except meat and special delicacies: truly it was like the great Mosaic jubilee of ancient times. In the following three years food was no less plentiful.

But alas! Since the beginning of time humankind has been forgetful of the benefits conferred by God and prone to evil; like a dog returning to its vomit or a pig wallowing in its mire, in many respects they broke their sworn agreements. . . .

At that time [1041], by the inspiration of divine grace, a pact was confirmed first in Aquitaine and then gradually throughout Gaul. According to this it was agreed, out of both love and fear of God, that from Wednesday evening to dawn on the following Monday no one might presume to seize anything by force from another, or take vengeance upon an enemy or even take surety from an oathtaker. Whoever acted against this public decree was either to pay for it with his life or be driven from his own country and the company of his fellow Christians. Moreover, all agreed that this should be called, in the vulgar tongue, the Truce of God, since it was not upheld by human sanctions alone, but also, as has frequently been demonstrated, by divine vengeance. Various madmen did not fear to break the pact, and immediately avenging divine wrath or the punishing sword of men fell upon them. This happened so often that the frequency of such events keeps me from enumerating these instances.

2

BISHOPS OF THE AUVERGNE

Canons of the Council of Le Puy

994

What kinds of violence were the Peace councils trying to curb? While there was variance regionally and over time as the movement developed, the concerns of the bishops of the Auvergne gathered at Le Puy at the end of the tenth century were fairly typical. Three general aims can be discerned in these and other canons: the protection of the church and its property; the protection of defenseless people (the unarmed, clergy, pil-

---

Cartulaire de Sauxillanges, ed. H. Doniol (Paris: F. Thibaud, 1864), 52–54; E. Magnou-Nortier, "La place du Concile du Puy (v. 994) dans l'évolution de l'idée de paix," *Mélanges offerts à Jean Dauvillier* (Toulouse: Centre d'histoire juridique méridionale, 1979), 499–500.

grims); and the protection of livestock and agricultural production. Also evident are some of the issues that would later be prominent in the reform movement—the clergy bearing arms, for example, and priests accepting payments for sacraments or offices (an abuse called simony).

In the name of God, and of the highest and indivisible Trinity, Wido bishop of Le Puy by the grace of God, to those awaiting the mercy of celestial piety, greetings and peace.

We wish all the faithful of God to know that upon seeing the evils that daily increase among the people, we gathered together the bishops Peter of Viviers, Wido of Valence, Bego of Auvergne, Raimund of Toulouse, Deusdedit of Rodez, Fredelo of Elne, and Lord Fulcran of Lodève, and Wido of Glandèves and many other bishops, princes, and nobles too numerous to name.

Because we know that without peace no one will see the Lord, in order that these may be sons of peace, in the name of the Lord we warn that in the dioceses ruled by these bishops as well as in the counties,

1. that from this hour forward, no man may invade the immunity[1] of a church;

2. that from the atrium outside a church or from a fortified enclosure of a monastery, no man knowingly may seize, either in these counties or dioceses, public horses, oxen, cows, male and female donkeys, the burdens they carry, nor the flocks of sheep, goats, pigs (the only exception being bishops collecting their rents or dues [*censum*]); nor may any man kill any of these, unless he and his followers were given a safe conduct to travel through the area—then they may receive them for sustenance.

3. Concerning the same [matter of protected animals and goods], no one may carry them off to his house, or lay siege to a castle or construct one, unless it is on his own land, either his own property [*allod*] or his fief, and under his command.

4. Clerics may not carry secular armaments.

5. No man may injure monks in any way, nor those who accompany them who do not carry arms (except the bishop or archdeacon because of their rents or dues [*censum*]).

---

[1]The author seems to be using *immunity* in the sense of a protected zone, exempt from incursions and exactions made by the more powerful members of the local community. Generally, an immunity is a grant, usually by a ruler, of exemption (from, for example, taxes or certain dues).

6. No man may take a male or female serf hostage seeking payment for their redemption, unless the serf is guilty of wrongdoing, or is one who tills or works land which is in dispute, or unless the serf is one of those from his own land or fief.

7. No one should dare to take the lands of ecclesiastics, bishops, canons, or monks, or to dishonor them with evil customs, unless he shall have acquired the lands through a lease from either a bishop or with the will of the brothers.

8. From this hour onward, no one should knowingly apprehend a merchant or despoil his goods.

9. We also prohibit that any layperson help himself to the burial fees or offerings of a church, or that any priest accept payment for baptism, which is a gift of the Holy Spirit.

If, indeed, there shall be any robber or scurrilous person who shall have broken this agreement and refused to abide by it, let him be excommunicated and anathematized and excluded from communion with the holy church of God until he makes satisfaction. If he does not make satisfaction and he dies, no priest may bury him and he may not be buried within a church. No priest may knowingly give communion to him and if any priest knowingly goes against this, he shall be removed from holy orders.

We pray and admonish that from this time, namely the middle of October, you will hold to this peace of God in good faith and free will, and that as a result you may merit the remission of your sins, under the protection of our Lord Jesus Christ who lives and reigns with the Father and the Holy Spirit.

Dagbert Archbishop of Bourges and Lord Theotbald, Archbishop of Vienne confirmed this agreement.

Monastic Reform

3

WILLIAM OF AQUITAINE

Foundation Charter of the Monastery of Cluny

910

Monastic renewal had been an important part of Carolingian attempts to reform the church, but the instability of the late ninth and tenth centuries provoked a new wave of monastic reform that was to have a more enduring legacy. The exact relation of monastic reform to the broader eleventh-century calls for ecclesiastical reform has been much debated. But many of the themes later central to the reform movements are evident in the reformed monasticism of the tenth century, and by the eleventh century these movements were intimately related. The monastery of Cluny, located in Burgundy, came to play a particularly prominent role. Founded in 910 by Duke William of Aquitaine, Cluny under its second abbot, Odo (927–942), became an active force for reform: Monks were sent out from Cluny to other monasteries in France and Italy in order to recall them to a strict observance of the Rule of St. Benedict. Just as it was William, a layman, who founded Cluny and gave it freedom from all ecclesiastical and secular lordship (including his own), usually it was the lay founders and patrons of monasteries who initiated renewal by giving a house over to the abbot of Cluny to be reformed. The independence of Cluny, especially the monks' freedom to elect their abbot, was considered a key factor in its success.

To all those sensibly considering the matter, it is clear that the providence of God has so provided for certain rich men, by means of their transitory possessions, that if they use them well, they may be able to

Select Historical Documents of the Middle Ages, trans. E. F. Henderson (London: George Bell & Sons, 1892), 329–33, revised and expanded from *Recueil des chartes de l'abbaye de Cluny,* ed. Auguste Bernard and Alexandre Bruel, 6 vols. (Paris: Imprimerie nationale, 1876–1903), 1: 124–28 (no. 112).

merit everlasting rewards. Indeed, the divine word reveals the possibility and urges everyone toward it, saying: "Man's wealth is the redemption of his soul" (Prov. 13:8). Therefore, I, William, count and duke by the grace of God, diligently pondering this, and desiring to provide for my own safety while I am still able, have considered it desirable—nay, most necessary—that from the temporal goods bestowed upon me I should give some little portion for the profit of my soul. Because, in fact, I seem to have grown wealthy in such things [temporal goods], lest perhaps I am confounded—and either in the end spend it all on the care of the body or rather find at the end that fate shall have swept it all away—I would rejoice to have reserved something for myself. This may happen by no cause, pretext, or way more fitting than according to the precept of Christ: "I make myself a friend of the poor" (Luke 16:9). And so that an act of this sort endures not just for a period of time but continuously, I would support at my own expense those having gathered in the monastic profession. Although I myself can not renounce the things of the world in such faith and hope, provided that I shall have taken under my protection those despising the world whom I think are just, "I receive the reward of the just" (Matt. 10:41).

Therefore, to all those living in the unity of faith in Christ and begging his mercy, who are his successors and will prevail until the end of time, let it be known that out of love of God and our savior Jesus Christ, I hand over from my own rule to the holy apostles, Peter, namely, and Paul, the possessions over which I hold sway: namely, the town of Cluny with the enclosure and demesne[2] manor, and the church in honor of St. Mary the mother of God and of St. Peter the prince of the apostles, together with all the things pertaining to it, the estates, indeed, the chapels, the serfs of both sexes, the vines, the fields, the meadows, the woods, the waters and their outlets, the mills, the incomes and their revenues, what is cultivated and what is not, all in their entirety. These properties are located in the county of Mâcon or thereabouts, each within its bounds. I, William and my wife Ingelberga, give all these things to the aforesaid apostles first for love of God, then for the soul of my lord, King Odo,[3] the souls of my father and mother, for me and my wife, for the safety of our souls and bodies,

---

[2]*demesne:* The lord's land.
[3]*King Odo:* Son of Robert the Strong, count of Paris, and king of the West Franks (888–98).

and also for [my sister] Ava who conceded some of these things to me in her will, and for the souls of our brothers and sisters, our nephews and all our relatives of both sexes, for those faithful to us who remain in our service, and also for the status and soundness of the catholic religion. Finally, just as we, with all Christians, are part of one body of charity and faith, so let this gift be made for all these of orthodox faith, past, present, and future.

I give these things, moreover, with this understanding: that in Cluny a regular monastery shall be constructed in honor of the holy apostles Peter and Paul, and that there the monks shall congregate and live according to the rule of St. Benedict, and that they shall possess, hold, have and order these same things for all time. [I stipulate this] so that the house of venerable prayer there may faithfully resound with prayers and supplications; and so that celestial conversation with all longing and deepest ardor may be pursued and sought after there; and so that diligent prayers, requests, and appeals may there be addressed to the Lord, as much for me as for all others, as is set out above. And let the monks themselves, together with all the aforesaid possessions, be under the power and dominion of the abbot Berno, who, as long as he shall live, shall preside over them regularly according to his knowledge and ability. But after his death, those same monks shall have power and permission to elect any one of their order whom they please as abbot and rector, following the rule promulgated by St. Benedict—in such wise that neither by intervention of our own or of any other power may they be impeded from making a purely canonical election. Every five years, moreover, the aforesaid monks shall pay to the church of the apostles at Rome ten shillings to supply candles to light the church; and they shall have the protection of those same apostles and the defense of the Roman pontiff; and those monks may, with their whole heart and soul, according to their ability and knowledge, build up the aforesaid place. We also wish that, in our own time and that of our successors, as opportunity and possibility provide, daily works of mercy for the poor, the indigent, strangers, and pilgrims be offered there with the greatest care. It seems good also to include in this testament that from this day forward, the monks gathered there may not be subjected to our own control or that of our relatives, to the authority of any royal dignity, or the yoke of any temporal power whatsoever. And, through God and all his saints, and by the awful day of judgment, I pray and warn that no one of the secular princes, no count, no bishop whatever, not the pontiff of the aforesaid

Roman see, shall invade the property of these servants of God, or alienate it, or diminish it, or exchange it, or give it as a benefice[4] to anyone, or constitute any prelate over them against their will. In order that such wickedness from all rash and unruly men be more effectively restrained, addressing such ones forcefully, I add this prayer. I beseech you, most holy apostles and princes of the earth, Peter and Paul, and you, pope of the Apostolic See, through the canonical and apostolic authority you received from God, cast out from the society of the sacred church of God and of eternal life, anyone who robs, invades, or tears apart these things which I give to you with a glad mind and resolute will! And be the caretakers and defenders of the aforesaid place of Cluny, the servants of God gathered there, and all their goods, on account of the clemency and mercy of our redeemer! If anyone, by chance, . . . may be tempted to strike in any way against this testament—which I had drawn up out of love for almighty God and veneration of the princes of the apostles, Peter and Paul—may he, first of all, incur the wrath of omnipotent God, and may God cast him out of the land of the living, and delete his name from the book of life. And may he be with those who say to the Lord God, "Leave us!" (Job 21:14) and with Dathan and Abiron, whom the earth gobbled with open mouth, and hell swallowed alive (Num. 16:1–35). May he incur eternal damnation as an ally of Judas, the traitor of the Lord, and having been cast out, held in eternal torment. And lest anyone, in the present time and to human eyes, seems to act against this testament with impunity, he shall know from experience in his own body the torments of future damnation, having been allotted the double ravaging of Heliodorus and Antiochus, of whom one, having been chastised with stinging lashes, barely escaped alive (2 Macc. 3:22–39) and the other, having been struck down by God's command, miserably perished with putrifying members and swarming worms (2 Macc. 9:1–11). . . . According to worldly law, anyone who shall have made any misrepresentation concerning these things shall be compelled by the judicial power to pay one hundred pounds of gold . . . Enacted publicly in the city of Bordeaux. I, William, commanded this act to be made and drawn up, and confirmed it with my own hand. [Then follow the confirmation of his wife, Ingelberga, and the names of 42 other witnesses]

---

[4]*benefice:* A gift or reward given in return for services. It could mean a fief, a grant of land to a vassal in return for military service, or the property attached to a church to support a cleric. Since William seems concerned about protecting the property from the predations of both secular and ecclesiastical lords, it could mean either.

Given 3 ides September [September 11], in the eleventh year of King Charles, 13th indiction. I, Oddo, priest, for the chancellor, wrote and signed this.

4

PETER DAMIAN

On the Life of the Hermit Romuald of Ravenna

1042

Although the Cluniac model was highly influential, the renewal of monastic life took many different forms. A particularly strong current in eleventh-century European monastic reform was the "eremitic monasticism" dominant in the eastern Mediterranean, particularly in the deserts of Egypt and Syria. This form of spiritual practice emphasized ascetic solitude rather than communal prayer. Hermits, as the practitioners of this type of monasticism were called, lived throughout Europe in the eleventh century, but they particularly flourished in Italy. The career of Saint Romuald of Ravenna (d. 1027) illustrates both the attractions of the eremitic life and the tendency for communities to form around inspirational hermits. Romuald eventually founded several monasteries for his disciples that combined eremitic solitude with communal labor and liturgies. This passage describes Romuald's entry into the eremitic life, after a brief period in the Benedictine monastery of Classe, and a small portion of his subsequent career. Peter Damian, who wrote about the life of Saint Romuald in 1042, was a monk and a relentless advocate of reform. An extremely ascetic personality, Damian lived most of his life in the hermitage of Fonte Avellana in the Apennine mountains of central Italy.

When Romuald noticed that some of his fellow monks [at Classe] were living rather slackly and that he was not going to be able to keep

---

Petri Damiani Vita beati Romualdi, chaps. 3–4, 31, 37, ed. G. Tabacco, Fonti per la storia d'Italia 94 (Rome: Istituto storico italiano per il Medio Evo, 1957), 19–21, 67–68, 77–78.

to the difficult path of perfection that he had set out for himself, he began to wonder what he should do and many conflicting thoughts boiled up inside him. Nevertheless, he would take it upon himself to reprove his brothers harshly for their way of life and often, to their embarrassment, he would invoke the precepts of their rule as support [for his criticisms]. Since he persisted in pointing out their vices, they began to think of murdering him. They did not take his reproaches to heart and refused to emend their lives, for they had no respect for the words of their junior, who was but a novice. . . .

[The other monks plot to kill Romuald by throwing him from an upper floor, but he is able to avoid the trap.]

Just when Romuald's desire for perfection was growing stronger day by day and he could find no peace, he heard about a certain holy man, by the name of Marin, who was living near Venice as a hermit. The permission of his abbot and brethren being readily granted, he set off by ship to this holy man and he decided with humble devotion to put himself under his direction. Indeed Marin, among his other virtues, was a man of great simplicity and purity. No one had taught him how to be a hermit; he had been inspired by the impulse of his own worthy desires. For years he subsisted on half a loaf of bread and a handful of beans three days of the week and on a little soup and wine for the other three, [fasting on the seventh day]. He sang the entire Psalter every single day. But since no one had taught him about the ordering of the solitary life—as Romuald himself afterward recounted with some mirth—he would often leave his cell with his disciple and walk up and down the hermitage singing psalms here and there, twenty under that tree, now thirty or forty under another. . . .

[Romuald left the company of Marin to help his father live a monastic life, and then he began to wander.]

Romuald stayed near Parenzo for three years. During the first year he built a monastery; for the next two he lived as a recluse. It was there that his God-given piety brought him to the summit of perfection so that, inspired by the Holy Spirit, he could foresee events and penetrate many of the hidden mysteries of the Old and New Testaments with the rays of his intelligence. For some time he had anxiously desired the gift of tears but no effort he made yielded the compunction of a contrite heart. One day, however, when he was singing the Psalms in his cell he fell upon the following verse: "I will give you understanding and teach you the way you should go; I will fix my eyes upon you" (Ps. 32 [31]:8). Immediately an abundance of tears welled up in his eyes and he received such illumination in the understanding of divine scripture that from that day forward, for the rest of his life and whenever he wanted, he could easily burst into tears and many mysteries of scripture were no longer hidden to him. . . .

Having left the Val de Castro with some of his disciples, Romuald went to the countryside around Orvieto where he built another monastery on land donated by Count Farolfo and with the support of many. So heartfelt was that holy man's longing to do good that he was never satisfied with what he achieved. As soon as he got one project going, he would rush off to start another, so that one might have thought that he wanted to make the whole world into a hermitage and everyone into monks. As it was, he snatched many away from the world, settling them in many holy places.

Clerical Celibacy and Simony

5

PETER DAMIAN

A Letter to Bishop Cunibert of Turin
1064

Peter Damian was an uncompromising advocate of ecclesiastical renewal. He served the cause of reform by attending councils and undertaking missions as a papal legate, but especially by writing. He carried on a voluminous correspondence, and the excerpts here are from a treatise-length letter he wrote to Bishop Cunibert of Turin in 1064.

To Sir Cunibert, the most reverend bishop, the monk Peter the sinner sends his humble service.

Peter Damian, Letter 112, *The Letters of Peter Damian,* trans. Owen J. Blum, in *The Fathers of the Church: Medieval Continuation* (Washington, D.C.: The Catholic University Press of America Press, 1989), 5: 258–59, 266–69, 270–71, 285.

It is the norm of true love and friendship that brothers should foster such mutual affection that if anything reproachful be found in either of them, one will not hide it from the other. Such urgency proves to be both useful and upright, for as it brings everything into the open, it repairs that which needs correction and safeguards what is conducive to their well-being by a pure and sincere exchange of love. And so it happens, that as the delinquent's fault is called to his attention, he who corrects amasses a greater amount of grace. Among the various virtues, venerable father, with which your holiness is adorned, I must say that one thing greatly displeases me, which, on the occasion of my visit to you, caused me to be very angry with you, and which now compels me to bring it up again in this letter. For you have been permissive toward the clerics of your diocese, whatever orders they might have received, allowing them to live with their wives as if they were married men. God forbid that in your great prudence you should be unaware that such a practice is obscene and opposed to ecclesiastical purity, contrary to the commands of the canons, and certainly offensive to all the norms promulgated by the holy Fathers. This is especially true, since these very clerics of yours are otherwise decent people and properly educated in the study of the arts. Indeed, when they met me, they appeared to shine like a choir of angels and like a distinguished senate of the Church.

But after I learned of the hidden discharge flowing from this disease, light was suddenly converted into darkness, and my joy was turned into sorrow, and I at once recalled this saying of the Gospel, "Alas for you, lawyers and Pharisees! You are like tombs covered with whitewash; they look well from the outside, but inside they are full of dead men's bones and all kinds of filth" (Matt. 23:27). How is it, father, that you watch out only for yourself, and that in regard to those for whom you must first give an account you are indolently asleep? Certainly, in other individuals productive chastity is not required; but in a bishop chastity is rightly considered unprofitable if it remains so sterile that it does not give birth to chastity in others. . . .

[Peter then goes through numerous scriptural passages and excerpts from the Fathers and church councils, requiring the chastity of the clergy.]

Therefore, since all the holy Fathers, who with the aid of the Holy Spirit fashioned the canons, without dissent unanimously concur that clerical chastity must be observed, what will await those who blaspheme against the Holy Spirit by satisfying their own carnal desires? Because of a flux of momentary passion, they earn the reward of burning in eternal fire that cannot be quenched. Now they wallow in the filth of impurity, but later, given over to the avenging flames, they will be rolled about in a flood of pitch and sulphur. Now, in the heat of passion, they are themselves a very hell, but then, buried in the depths of eternal night, they must forever suffer the torments of a savage inferno. In themselves they now feed the fires of lust, but then with their inmost beings they will nourish the flames of a fire that is never extinguished. Oh, unhappy and pitiful men! By observing the law of their putrid flesh which awaits devouring worms, they despise the laws of him who came down from heaven and reigns over the angels. And so, in the words of the prophet, the Lord says to the reprobate, "You have preferred your body to me" (Ezek. 23:35), as if to say, "You placed your bodily pleasure before the law, and despised the commands of my precepts." Surely, the law of the human body is contrary to the law of God. Hence the Apostle says, "I perceive that there is in my bodily members a different law, fighting against the law that my reason approves and making me a prisoner to the law of sin that is in my members" (Rom 7:23).

They, therefore, prefer their body to God, who by despising the rule of divine law, obey the pleasures of their own desires; and in unleashing the reins of lust, transgress the norms of restraint imposed upon them. They ignore the fact that for every fleeting enjoyment of intercourse they prepare a thousand years in hell, and those who now ignite the flame of lust, will then be consumed in avenging fire. But for those who wallow in the filth of wanton pleasure, how can they dare in their pernicious security to participate in the sacrament of the saving Eucharist, since through Moses the Lord said to his priests, "Any man of your descent who while unclean approaches the holy gifts which the Israelites hallow to the Lord shall be cut off from the presence of the Lord" (Heb. 10:1). And then the text continues, "No man descended from Aaron who suffers from a malignant skin disease, or has a discharge, shall eat of the holy gifts until he is cleansed" (Lev. 22:4). But if he who because of some bodily illness was afflicted with uncleanness of any kind was not permitted to eat of the food offerings, how can he who is willingly contaminated by sexual pleasure offer the sacraments to God? . . .

Therefore, since intercourse in marriage is preempted by prayer for laymen, how can it be reasonably permitted to clerics serving the sacred altar? How can they ever find time to live as married men, when they are never free from the duty of ecclesiastical service? For the Apostle says to the Corinthians, "The unmarried man cares for the Lord's business; his aim is to please the Lord. But the married man cares for worldly things; his aim is to please his wife" (1 Cor. 7:32–33). And so he who is dedicated to divine service must always be intent on God's business and should not be distracted by carnal affection. But how can he be solicitous and always attentive to his Maker, when his heart is closely bound to his wife? "Do you know," he says, "that your bodies are limbs and organs of Christ?" (1 Cor. 6:15). And omitting many things which the same Apostle says on this theme, lest I cause you to be bored, let me at least cite the following, "Do you not know that your body is a temple of the indwelling Holy Spirit?" (1 Cor. 6:19). Elsewhere he says of this temple, "Anyone who destroys God's temple will himself be destroyed by God" (1 Cor. 3:17).

If, therefore, not only the soul but our very body, which is seen and touched externally, is without doubt the temple of the Holy Spirit, how can we say that he who is forbidden to have carnal intercourse, does not destroy the temple of God when in his wanton lust he makes himself a prostitute, rejects the Holy Spirit whose seal he bears, and in his stead welcomes the spirit of impurity? . . .

But now the ministers of the Church, who have Christ as their master, him who was crucified, do not shudder at living to enjoy their bodily pleasures, neighing after that to which the desires of the flesh entice them, as the Lord says through Jeremiah, "I gave them all they needed, yet they preferred adultery, and haunted the brothels; each neighs after another man's wife, like a well-fed and lusty stallion" (Jer. 23:15). And again, "For prophet and priest alike are defiled; I have come upon the evil they are doing even in my own house. This is the very word of the Lord" (Jer. 23:11). . . . How imprudently presumptuous, moreover, is their boldness, that while unable to escape from this foul contagion, they are still unwilling to abandon the practice of their ministry in which they so unworthily persist, since the Lord says to them through Isaiah, "Whenever you come into my presence— who asked you for this? No more shall you trample my courts. The offer of your gifts is useless, the reek of sacrifice is abhorrent to me" (Isa. 1:12–13). . . .

How much better it would be for these men to withdraw from exercising their orders than provoke God to use the sword of his anger against them; how much more discreet to depart and not serve at Christ's altars than to pollute thereby their presence? . . .

In the plenary synod it was Pope Leo of blessed memory, who decreed that whenever these damnable women, living with priests as their mistresses, were found living within the walls of the city of Rome, they were to be condemned from then on to be slaves of the

Lateran [papal] palace. I have also decided to publicize this salutary law, so replete with justice and equity, throughout all dioceses, so that after first hearing the decree of the Apostolic See, every bishop may acquire as slaves of his diocese all the women in his territory that he finds living in sacrilegious union with priests. It is clearly a matter of justice, that those who have stolen the ministry of the servants of God at the holy altar, should at least reimburse the bishop with their service after forfeiting their civil rights. . . .

And so, venerable father, bravely arm yourself for this conflict between chastity and lust. Unsheathe the sword of the Spirit and fatally wound this violent impurity, raging in your diocese, that as a valiant soldier you may snatch the spoils from the bloody hands of this invader, and be worthy of bearing the banners of victory to the Author of chastity himself.

6

ANDREW OF STRUMI

Description of the Preaching of Ariald in Milan

ca. 1075

The purity of the clergy was not an issue that interested only monks and popes. All people depended on the clergy for the sacraments that were believed to aid salvation. Thus, many laypeople felt tremendous anxiety about the virtue of their local priests. Were sacraments administered by sinful priests valid? If an impure priest baptized your child, distributed Holy Communion, or administered last rites, was the grace that the sacrament was supposed to impart impaired? Around 1056 a popular movement against immoral priests began in the northern Italian city of Milan. Its leaders were educated elites, both clerics and laymen, but its followers were drawn largely from the lower classes. Indeed, the name given to the movement, Pataria, and to its supporters, Patarenes, probably derives from pattari, the term for rag-sellers or used clothing vendors.

Andrew of Strumi, *Vita sancti Arialdi,* chaps. 5–6, ed. F. Baethgen, in *Monumenta Germaniae historica, Scriptores,* vol. 30, part 2 (Leipzig: Hiersemann, 1934), 1052.

The earliest leader, Ariald of Carimate, was from a Milanese family of the lesser nobility. He studied in the finest schools of the time, was ordained a priest, and became a canon in the cathedral chapter of Milan. In 1056 he began preaching against the immorality of the clergy, and this precipitated almost two decades of struggle in the city over local ecclesiastical customs, reform, and relations with Rome. The conflicts were often violent. Ariald was captured in 1065 by some of the archbishop's knights, who tortured, mutilated, and murdered him. In 1067 Pope Alexander II declared him a martyr. This account of his earliest preaching was written in about 1075 by Andrew of Strumi, a priest and monk who was in Milan during the beginning of the Patarene movement.

[Ariald was saying . . .] "Of course, that great, eternal, and living light [Jesus] left two means on earth through which all those who ought to be enlightened were and remained so for all eternity, so too those who still ought to be enlightened, as well as those who already shall have been. Do you want to know what these means were? They were, namely, the word of God and the life of the learned. About the word of God, which is light, listen not to my testimony but to that of the Psalmist: 'The bright precept of the Lord,' he said, 'gives light to the eyes' (Ps. 18:9). And again, 'your word is a lamp unto my feet' (Ps. 118:105). About the life of the learned, which ought to be light, let this truth be clearly manifest to you through him in his words: 'You,' he said, 'are the light of the world.' And, continuing, he added, 'so let your light shine forth among men so that they might see your good works and glorify your father in heaven' (Matt. 5:14, 16). Accordingly from these [means], the Lord put one before those and the other before you. He chose those, indeed, to whom he gave knowledge of scripture, as his ministers; established that they were always to live in the light of his bright word; and ordained that their life be your reading, you who cannot read letters. But with that enemy of the human race instigating and, at the same time, working through our negligence and sin, by turning themselves away, those ones lost their light and you lost yours. Moreover, in order to more surely delude you that same enemy, who took away the truth of holiness from them, let them in their outward appearance have the semblance of holiness. Sighing, I say this not to disgrace you, but to caution you. Have you not returned to that same blindness that caused Christ mercifully to descend from heaven to liberate humankind? If, therefore, the human race before his coming was, as we say, blind — because it mistook lies for truth — whoever now makes a similar mistake, does he not end up in the same condition? For just as the deceived believe in wooden and stone gods, so you believe your priests, who are entirely false, to be real. How are you able to know this? Are you willing to know how? We are in the shadows; so that we might know this clearly, let us go into the light. To what light? To the word of God, of course. Behold, Christ said, 'You who serve me, follow me.' Which is clearly to say, 'no one may serve me, of course, unless he follows me.' I know that you know about the lives of your priests and Christ goes on about that. Listen to what he may say and then you may know more fully whether these are his ministers or (more likely) his adversaries. Behold, Christ proclaims: 'Learn from me because I am gentle and humble of heart' (Matt. 11:29). And, again, he said of himself: 'The Son of Man does not have a place to rest his head' (Matt. 8:20). And again, 'Blessed are the poor in spirit since theirs is the kingdom of heaven' (Matt. 5:3). On the other hand, consider your priests who are more rich in worldly goods, more illustrious in building towers and houses, more puffed up with honors, and more beautiful in their soft, choice garments: these are considered more blessed. Indeed, these, as you know, openly take wives just like laymen, pursue debauchery just like the most wicked laymen, and to top off this impiety, they are more powerful for being less weighed down with earthly labor since, of course, they are living off what was given to God. Christ, on the contrary, sought and desired such purity in his ministers that he condemned the evil of debauchery not only in their works but also in their hearts, saying: 'He who shall have looked lustfully at a woman has already copulated with her in his heart' (Matt. 5:23). Look into your hearts, dearest ones, look and learn to embrace the true and reject the false. I, indeed, attempted to lead these ones again into their light, but I was not able. So that I might lead you back into your light, I came here. And either I shall accomplish this, or for your safety I am prepared to offer my soul to the sword."

Now, while that man of God was saying these and many similar things, just about all the people were so inflamed by his words that those once venerated as ministers of Christ were proclaimed enemies of God and deceivers of souls. . . .

7

ARNULF OF MILAN

On the Patarenes

ca. 1072–1077

Not everyone, however, thought Ariald and his followers were saintly. Another contemporary, Landulf Senior, wrote that Ariald was motivated "not by divine inspiration, but by human failings," chief among them pride and the desire for revenge against other clerics. A less polemical, but still critical, view of the Patarenes was given by Arnulf in his Deeds of the Archbishops of Milan *(written ca. 1072–1077). Scholars are divided over whether the author was a cleric or a layman, but he was clearly from the city's high nobility and defended the distinctive ecclesiastical traditions of the city. This is his account of the preaching of Ariald's associate Landulf Cotta and its effects.*

[Landulf exhorted his listeners]: "How can the blind lead the blind without both ending up in some pit? The priests, deacons, and other ministers of the altar, in fact, abandon themselves to every sort of lechery, even, sadly to the heresy of simony. From the moment they fall into these sins, they should be deprived of their offices. Because of this, from now on you should avoid such clerics and their sacraments if you want to obtain your salvation from our Savior: their sacrifices have the same value as dog feces and their churches are like animal stalls. The goods of these reprobates have been condemned and permission given to all to pillage them, whether they be within or outside of the city. I myself committed such regretful acts. What is far worse is that such unworthy wretches should offend the king of heaven by offering communion. Now, however, I am doing penance, heaping up future goods [in heaven]. Imitate me, my dear ones, and thus walk our own road."

Having said these things and many others, which the limits of human memory keep me from recalling, the people, ever avid for new

Arnulf of Milan, *Gesta archiepiscoporum Mediolanensium,* book 3, chaps. 11–12, ed. L. C. Bethmann and W. Wattenbach, in *Monumenta Germaniae historica, Scriptores,* vol. 8 (Hannover: Hahn, 1848), 19–20.

things, were excited with no little zeal against the clergy. Some believed they were doing God's will, while others were motivated by avarice. This Landulf and his accomplice Ariald whipped up their fervor like this for days on end, following every favorable wind, ever adding new and unheard of charges, according to the vulgar tastes of the crowd. Several times church authorities tried to put the brakes on their temerity, pointing out how the sacred scriptures and canon law contradicted their views. Disdaining such sources, they pressed on. On one solemn feast day they went so far as to assemble a great throng in front of the church and then [entering] violently cast out of their choir stalls all the clergy singing the psalms, chasing them into corners and other parts.

Later, more astutely, they had an edict written on the duty of the clergy to be chaste, and although it was based entirely on secular rather than canon law, they forced all the Milanese clergy and laity to sign it. Meanwhile, bands of looters, having already destroyed many buildings in the city, scoured the parishes, sacking the homes of clerics and carrying off all they owned.

8

POPE GREGORY VII

A Letter to Adela, Countess of Flanders
November 10, 1076

The genesis of this letter of Pope Gregory VII is unclear, but its message is not. Most likely the papal legate Hubert, mentioned at the end of the letter, had briefed the pope on conditions in Flanders, and this letter was meant to reassure the countess. Many nobles like Adela not only feared for their own salvation but felt it their duty to act for the good of their subjects by ensuring a proper order in their local Christian church. Moreover, as this letter makes clear, church leaders actively solicited the help of the lay rulers in the work of reform. Particularly interesting in

Das Register Gregors VII, 4.10, ed. E. Caspar, in *Monumenta Germaniae historica, Epistolae selectae,* vol. 2, part 1 (Berlin: Weidmann, 1920–23; rpt. Munich, 1990), 309.

this missive is the fact that the pope encourages a laywoman to reject the advice of a priest and high-ranking ecclesiastical official.

Bishop Gregory, servant of the servants of God, to Countess Adela of Flanders—greeting and apostolic blessing.

We have heard that some of your people doubt whether priests or deacons or other ministers of the altar who persist in fornication ought to celebrate the mass. To these we respond, following the authority of the holy fathers, that unchaste servants of the altar should, under no circumstances, celebrate the mass. Rather, they are to be expelled from the choir until they show themselves worthy of the fruits of repentance.

Therefore, by apostolic authority, we admonish you to let none of those who persist in this evil celebrate the sacred mysteries, but from wherever you can, seek out for the celebration of the mass those who serve God chastely. Having expelled those [fornicating clerics] from every ecclesiastical benefice, do not listen to a word Archdeacon Hubert [of Thérouanne] says or follow any of his advice, because, as I have heard, he has fallen into heresy through his crooked disputes and been publically convicted at Montreuil by Hubert, legate of this Holy Roman See.

9

HUMBERT OF SILVA CANDIDA

On Simony

1058

A monk of the reformed monastery of Moyenmoutier in Lotharingia, Humbert came to Rome with Bruno of Toul (Pope Leo IX), who made him cardinal of Silva Candida in 1051. He remained an extremely influential figure in Roman reforming circles until his death a decade

Humberti cardinalis Libri Tres Adversus Simoniacos, book 1, chap. 4, ed. E. G. Robison (Ann Arbor: University Microforms International, 1972), 18–20.

later. His Three Books against the Simoniacs, *written in 1058 just after the death of Pope Stephen IX, addressed a highly controversial issue in the practical enactment of reforms. Were priests, who were innocent of simony but who had been ordained by bishops guilty of having bought their offices, truly priests and capable of transmitting the grace of the sacraments? Or did they need to be ordained anew? In the 1050s, this issue deeply divided reformers. All agreed that simony was a grave sin and a heresy, but was it so serious a heresy that it nullified the sacraments (especially that of ordination) that had been administered by the sinner? The practical implications of this issue were enormous. Humbert implied that any sacrament administered by a simoniacal bishop or even by those he had ordained must be performed again. In the end, Humbert's position was not adopted by the church, but it reveals why the abuses that the reformers battled elicited strong feelings, radical calls for change, and violence.*

... Finally, I ask that the simonists, their intimate servants, and faithful followers wake up, so that seeing how much ruin that first simonist [Simon Magus[5]] caused and what a fall he took in the end, they might reconsider and, even if late, acknowledge where they may fall and that by persisting they may incur a penalty not twice his, but more than a thousand times. [They merit this] since they have dared to believe themselves priests through money paid or [they believed themselves] able to hold, deserve, or give an ecclesiastical office to anyone, whether free or at a price. They were in no way able to obtain through payment what I acquired [through ordination], objecting as the Prince of the Apostles did to Simon: "You don't have any part in this" (Acts 8:21).

In comparison with this presumption, the error of Magus—who thought only that the gift of God could be bought—was more pardonable than the error of these who believe, trust, and even assert that since their payment was accepted that they may pass on the gift of

---

[5]*Simon Magus:* A man from Samaria who, in the Acts of the Apostles 8:4–24, marveled at the miracles the apostles were working and offered them money to lay hands on him to give them these wonder-working powers. In this scriptural account, the apostle Peter rebuked him for thinking he could buy God's gift, and Simon was penitent. But in the apocryphal "Acts of Saint Peter"—one of many early Christian texts not incorporated into the canonical New Testament but influential in early Christian communities— Simon supposedly followed the apostles Peter and Paul to Rome, trying at every turn to frustrate their missionary efforts with witchcraft. Thus Simon Magus came to be known in the early church as the first obdurate heretic and the "Father of Heresies."

God to anyone. For if they did not believe this, then they themselves would not, as they boast, be able to be bishops with us, and would not continue to usurp their office and pass on their own perdition and damnation more than any ordination or consecration of episcopal ministry. If, however, they do believe this, then they clearly are heretics, far worse than that one [Simon Magus] who first thought or conjectured as much. If, indeed, they do not believe this, why do they presume to bestow office? Why do they not recognize that they cannot concede to others in ministry what they do not themselves possess?

In this too they are clearly heretics and they despair, or rather, of course, in the perverse hope of the accursed, they may add daily blasphemies to his first blasphemy against the Holy Spirit, making themselves worse than their master. That one [Simon Magus] after being rebuked did not believe himself to have received the gift of God (namely, the Holy Spirit) and because of this he did not lay hands on anyone. . . . That one was evil because he offered money for this [gift of God], but these are worse because they not only offered but actually gave it constantly. That one was evil because, not even a year having passed since his conversion, he fell away once and for all through this sacrilege. But how much worse are these ones because, having received the faith of Christ in the wombs of their mothers, from boyhood all the way to old age they grasped after nothing other than planning or plundering. That one was wicked because, not having been reproached or warned, he was filled with regret. More wicked are these because incorrigible and unrepentant, moved by no rebuke or admonition, they would not relinquish conferring office or the place they had arrogated to themselves and subject themselves to the yoke of penance — if by chance losing so many along with themselves and infecting the church of Christ with the contagion of damnation may ever be forgiven. That one was bad because he undertook such a deed when hardly a year had passed since the suffering of our Lord. How much worse are these because a thousand years or more after Magus was condemned and rebuked, as if having been made bolder by the examples of innumerable condemned ones, they do not desist in perpetrating such a crime but even go beyond their master in persevering in the fault and believing, teaching, and acting against the clear teaching of truth, which is Christ, they rely on themselves to give and receive the Holy Spirit not freely, protesting this teaching "what you received freely, give freely" (Matt. 10:8).

Hence it is evident that those who did not seek to receive the Spirit of truth freely, received it not at all. What then, I ask, did they receive? Without doubt, they give the Spirit of lies, whether freely or not, to anyone upon whom they lay hands: they are able to give nothing other than what they received because the grape may not be harvested either from the thistles of a fig or from a bramble-bush. Finally, unless grace is freely received, it is not grace and can not properly be called grace. Simonists do not receive freely what they receive. Therefore, they do not receive grace, which is especially at work in ecclesiastical orders. If they do not receive it, they do not have it. If they do not have it, they can not give what they do not have to anyone either freely or for payment. What, therefore, do they give? Certainly, what they have. What, indeed, do they have? The Spirit of lies, especially. How do we prove this? Because if the Spirit of truth (by giving evidence of the truth from which it proceeds) is received freely, what is not received freely without doubt is proven to be the spirit of lies.

10

PETER DAMIAN

On Simony

1052

The position the church ultimately took on the issue of ordinations by simoniacal bishops was articulated by Peter Damian in a letter he wrote to Henry, archbishop of Ravenna, in the summer of 1052. It was later revised and came to be known as the Liber gratissimus. *Peter had a personal interest in the issue: He himself had been ordained by a simoniacal bishop, a fact that he revealed in the letter. His theological solution was derived from St. Augustine, who faced similar questions about the efficacy of sacraments during the Donatist Schism in the early fifth century.*

That the gift of God is not defiled by impurity of its ministers.

If, in fact, the brightness of the visible sun is not affected by the darkness and dankness of the grave, if it is not defiled by filth from the sewers, is there any wonder that the most high and infinite Spirit

Die Briefe des Petrus Damiani, Teil 1: Nr. 1–40, letter no. 40, ed. K. Reindel (Munich: Monumenta Germaniae historica, 1983), 421–23.

should touch ever so lightly with his splendor the dark and squalid hearts of certain men, and still remain as clean and pure as he was? Anyone who consecrates, therefore, and is guilty of any crime—whether he is proud, or lustful, whether he is a murderer, or even a simonist—he is, indeed, tainted and undoubtedly mired in deadly leprosy, but the gift of God that passes through him is sullied by no one's corruption, is not infected by anyone's disease. That which flows through the minister is pure, and passes to a fertile soil, clean and clear. Holy Church, to be sure, is a garden of delights, a spiritual paradise, watered by a stream of celestial gifts. Let us assume, therefore, that bad priests are like stone canals; in such stone conduits water makes nothing grow until it flows through them and spills out into fertile fields. Although the passing of time should successively yield many corrupt priests, so that both those who ordain and those who are ordained are found equally unworthy, this living fountain is, nevertheless, not impeded from flowing through the glade of the church to the end of time, and from this fountain not only the priestly order but also all who are reborn in Christ drink the cup of salvation. Through priests, to be sure, baptism and holy oil are given to us, and by ecclesiastics alone the sacraments are administered. If, therefore, the wickedness of priests were able to inhibit divine gifts, then certainly their faults would make it necessary for the whole human race to forego divine benefits.

But if from faithful ministers men should receive these heavenly gifts, but from fallen ones they obtained nothing, they would necessarily attribute the cause and force behind their own salvation not to God but to priests. God forbid that an evil servant should be able to harm me when, without doubt, the master is good; or a malicious herald, where the judge is benevolent! The dove [i.e., the Holy Spirit] should be neither terrified nor disgusted at the ministry of certain foul individuals, provided that he alone upon whom he descends in his fullness [i.e., Christ] possesses the supremacy of consecration. For the unity of the church is established on this principle, that Christ retained as his own the power of consecrating and did not transfer his right to any of the ministers of consecration. For if consecration were to proceed from the worthiness or the virtue of the priest, it would obviously not belong to Christ at all. Although a bishop imposes hands and by the ministry committed to him recites the words of blessing, it is certainly Christ who consecrates and sanctifies by the hidden power of his majesty. So it was that a divine voice commanded Moses: "Say this to Aaron and his sons: 'This is how you are to bless the sons of Israel. You shall say to them: May the Lord bless you and keep you. May the Lord show his face to you and have mercy on you. May the Lord turn his face to you and give you peace.'" And then he continued: "You will invoke my name over the sons of Israel and I will bless them" (Num. 6:23–27). It is, therefore, the role of the priest to invoke God's name over those who are to be consecrated, but it is proper only to God to bless them inwardly. The external rites of consecration are clearly granted to the minister, but the efficacy of consecration itself is reserved solely to the Lord. For this reason the Lord said in Exodus, "It is I, the Lord, who sanctify you." Therefore, if it is the Lord who sanctifies, why should we fear that the fault of some servant who deserves punishment might stand in the way?

Canonical or "Free" Election

11

GERHARD OF AUGSBURG

How Ulrich Became Bishop of Augsburg
ca. 993

and

BERNO OF REICHENAU

How Ulrich Became Bishop of Augsburg
ca. 1030

Reformers believed that clerics, particularly bishops, had obtained their offices in other illicit ways besides simony. They generally saw lay influence as corrupting and tried to limit it by calling for a return to "canonical election." This phrase meant, in the case of a bishop, that he should be elected "by clergy and people," but no exact procedure had ever been

---

Gerhard von Augsburg, *Vita sancti Uodalrici. Die älteste Lebensbeschreibung des heiligen Ulrich,* ed. Walter Berschin and Angelika Häse (Heidelberg: Universitätsverlag C. Winter, 1993), 96–97; Berno of Reichenau, *Vita sancti Udalrici,* chap. 4, in *Patrologia cursus completus,* Series Latina, ed. J. P. Migne, 221 vols. (Paris: Garnier, 1844–64), 142: 1188.

defined. Did this mean that the clergy and people of a diocese confirmed by acclamation an individual put forward by the reigning bishop? This was how Saint Augustine became bishop of Hippo in 395. When the clergy and people joyfully received a candidate sent by a king or emperor, was this bishop elected "by clergy and people"? Which clerics and which "people" had the right to elect a bishop? We can get some sense of what reformers wanted (and what they didn't want) from two different versions of the life of Saint Ulrich, bishop of Augsburg (923–973). The earliest life of Ulrich was written between 983 and 993 by a contemporary, Gerhard, provost of the cathedral chapter of Augsburg. It most likely represents how Ulrich actually became bishop and includes the feudal ritual of offering homage or fidelity (which is not specified) by placing one's hands in the hands of the king. This life was updated and revised around 1030 by Berno, abbot of Reichenau and an advocate of reform. The different version he gives of how Ulrich became bishop reflects reform sensibilities. Note, however, that the king also had a role in Berno's rendition. The author alludes in his account to a hermit's prophecy that Ulrich would not stay in the monastery of Reichenau but would go east to serve God as a bishop.

Gerhard of Augsburg

Indeed, fifteen years later, when Bishop Hiltine [of Augsburg] died, Ulrich was brought to the attention of King Henry through the efforts of his nephew Duke Burchard and other relatives. They informed his majesty of the bishop's demise and asked him to concede the episcopal office to Ulrich. Considering his lordly stature and ascertaining his knowledge of doctrine, Henry gave his assent to their petition. According to royal custom, he received Ulrich's hands in his and conferred on him the episcopal office (*munere pontificatus*). These solemn acts having been completed, they parted from the king and returned to Augsburg in high spirits. Arriving in the city, they placed Ulrich in command of the diocese according to the royal edict investing him with full authority. During the following Christmas season, on the feast of the Holy Innocents, his ordination was completed with the customary rite.

Berno of Reichenau

After fifteen years, God willed that Hiltine leave the world in order that those things once said about his servant Ulrich might be fulfilled through the prayers of the faithful. The entire clergy and people acting in one accord, and King Henry consenting to their will in this matter, that holy man of God [Ulrich] assumed the episcopal throne in that city.

12

King Dagobert Invests Saint Omer
11th Century

Investiture was the ceremonial bestowal of the symbols of an office or honor on the new incumbent. In the case of bishops, the chief symbols bestowed were the crozier—a sort of shepherd's crook that represented episcopal authority—and a ring that symbolized their marriage to their see. Over the early Middle Ages kings frequently invested bishops. King Dagobert, pictured here, is believed to have appointed Omer to the see of Thérouenne in 637. This manuscript illumination, depicting the king investing the saintly bishop with his crozier, was made in the eleventh century. Although investiture could be related to uncanonical electoral practices (kings simply choosing bishops), it didn't necessarily preclude "free election." A bishop could be freely elected and then accept investiture from his king. Monarchs were attached to the rite because the patrimonies of many sees included royal estates granted as fiefs, and they expected the bishop to promise them fidelity in return for these lands—as Bishop Ulrich did (see Document 11).

King Dagobert Invests Saint Omer.
Courtesy of the Bibliothèque de l'agglomération de St-Omer. MS 698 fol. 7.

13

ANNALES ROMANI

Description of the Synod of Sutri
ca. 1046

and

BONIZO OF SUTRI

Description of the Synod of Sutri
ca. 1085

In the early eleventh century, the papacy was still very much controlled by Roman noble families. Those who believed that church reform was crucial considered the condition of the papacy a key problem. The question was how to wrest the throne of Saint Peter from Roman factions. This was ultimately accomplished between 1046 and 1048 through the intervention of King Henry III. When the king arrived in Italy in 1046, he found a messy three-way schism in progress. Since Henry wanted to be crowned emperor, it was critical that the pope who crowned him be unquestionably legitimate. He convened a synod (council) at Sutri to handle the schism. The German bishop, Suidger of Bamberg, whom Henry ultimately appointed pope (and who took the name Clement II), bestowed the imperial crown but didn't live long afterward. When Henry raised Bishop Bruno of Toul as Pope Leo IX in December 1048, however, the reformers finally gained the upper hand in Rome. The first account of these events comes from a roughly contemporary chronicle recorded in the city of Rome, the Annales Romani. *The second one gives more details, but it was written almost four decades later (ca. 1085) by Bonizo of Sutri. Bonizo was born about the time the council took place and therefore came of age in a very different church. He was an ardent reformer, attended many of the reform councils in Rome, and died combating abuses in the diocese of Piacenza. (His adversaries blinded and maimed*

Annales Romani, in *Monumenta Germaniae historica, Scriptores,* vol. 5, 468–69; Bonizo of Sutri, *Liber ad amicum,* book 5, ed. E. Dümmler, in *Monumenta Germaniae historica, Libelli de lite,* vol. 1 (Hannover: Hahn, 1891), 584–86.

*him in 1089; he died of his injuries shortly thereafter.) Although highly
polemical, Bonizo's account of his times is important because it covers
the most intense years of conflict over reform. Both accounts mention the
title of* patricius, *a Byzantine honorific bestowed by Pope Leo III on Pippin and Charlemagne to acknowledge their role as protectors of the Holy
See. Although the title originally entailed no rights or duties, its association with western emperors who tended to intervene in papal affairs led
to the idea in the late eleventh century that the* patricius *could create
popes.*

Annales Romani

In this year [1046] a great uprising occurred in Rome and a huge
crowd deposed the pope [Benedict IX]. . . . After this was done, a
battle broke out between the Romans and those living beyond the
Tiber, so that the Romans laid siege to Trastevere[6] for seven days in
January. The Romans were finally put to flight by counts from the
hill—namely, Gerard son of Rainerius, and his many knights—who
were faithful [*fideles*] to the aforesaid pontiff. . . . Then all the Romans
gathered together and elected John, Bishop of Sabina, as pope, who
took the name Silvester [III]. He held the see only 49 days and then
they re-enthroned Pope Benedict [IX]. But Benedict, not being able to
endure the Roman people, on the 1st of May renounced the office of
the papacy in writing to his godfather John, archpriest of San Giovanni
in Porta Latina, who took the name Gregory [VI]. He held the see for
a year, seven months, and twenty days.

Henry, most victorious king by the grace of God, having heard re-
ports of this unheard of controversy, came to Italy with great strength
and a huge army. When he arrived at the city of Sutri, he called the
Roman clergy along with Pope Gregory to meet with him. He ordered
a special synod to be held in the holy church of Sutri and there, lawfully and canonically, he sat in judgment upon Bishop John of Sabina,
called Silvester; the archpriest John, called Gregory; and the aforementioned Pope Benedict. Pointing out the relevant canons to the holy
and religious bishops gathered there, he condemned all three to perpetual anathema. Through God's mercy, the pious and gracious King
Henry then called together the multitude of the Roman people in the
basilica of blessed Peter prince of the apostles, and together with the
bishops, abbots, and entire clergy of Rome, celebrated another holy

---

[6]*Trastevere:* The neighborhood just south of Saint Peter's basilica, on the other side
of the Tiber from the most ancient part of Rome.

and glorious synod on the vigil of Christmas, at which he appointed an admirable, holy, and generous man [Suidger of Bamberg] as pontiff of the holy Roman church with the name Clement [II]. On Christmas day, that king was then crowned by his holy and gracious pope, and the entire city of Rome was filled with joy, the Roman church was exalted and glorified, that so great a heresy was thus eradicated through God's mercy. Moreover, the most serene prince, seeing that it was the will of the entire Roman people, placed on his own head the circlet with which the Romans from antiquity crowned their *patricius* and with one accord bestowed this title on the emperor. They also conceded to him the appointment of popes and the temporalities [*regalia*] of their deceased bishops. The kindly pontiff, along with the Romans and religious fathers, ordained, confirmed, and enacted that no one may be consecrated without first receiving investiture from the king: just as Pope Hadrian and other popes had confirmed through bestowal of the privilege, so let this patrician privilege be in the power of King Henry now and of future kings.

Bonizo of Sutri

[King Henry III] was extremely wise and a very devout Christian. At the beginning of his reign he quickly defeated and subdued the raging Magyars. Then, having duly pacified the realm, he resolved to go to Italy. Messengers coming from the city of Rome, however, slowing him extraordinarily, reported troubles going on there. For, as we mentioned above, the leading nobles *[capitanei]* of Rome, and chiefly the Tusculan clan, were then pillaging the Roman church. Since the office of *patricius* was vacant, indeed they seemed themselves by hereditary right to possess the papacy.

[Bonizo then recounts that in 1032, Pope John XIX died. He had been a member of the Tusculan family that had dominated the papacy for 30 years. A candidate from a rival noble family, the Crescenti, then became pope with the name Benedict IX.]

... [that one] perpetrated many sordid adulterous affairs and, with his own hands, even homicides. When, however, he wanted to marry his cousin, the daughter namely of Gerard of Saxo, [the father] refused to give her to him unless he renounced the papal office. So he [Benedict] bestowed it on that priest John [Gratian], who was believed to be quite deserving, and through his counsel, damned himself and renounced the papacy. That advice would have been quite praiseworthy, except that it was followed by an extremely sordid sin. For the same priest [John], about which we reported above, having accepted this opportunity, was seduced by impious bribery, disgraceful venality, and he compelled the entire Roman people by giving huge amounts of money, to swear allegiance to him. Thus he ascended to the papal dignity; they called him Gregory [VI]. After these events had transpired, Gerard of Saxo along with other leading nobles *[capitanei]* took it upon themselves to elect a certain bishop of Sabina pope and he took the name of Silvester [III]. Hearing this, [certain relatives of Benedict encouraged him], having been deceived by the hope of having a wife, to return to the height of the papal office.

But who was a source of help to us through so many calamities, except that evangelical voice that strengthened the apostle, saying: "I prayed for you, Peter, that your faith not fail you" (Luke 22:32)? Truly and certainly the faith of Peter did not fail, and the faith of the Roman church may never fail in eternity. Thus, God stirred up the spirit of a certain Roman archdeacon named Peter into a very great and powerful storm. Gathering bishops, cardinals, clerics and monks, men and women, all of them touched deeply by the fear of God, he withdrew himself from communion with the aforesaid invader [of the Holy See]. And led by the zeal of God, like that Jewish priest Onias (2 Macc. 4:4), he crossed the Alps, went to the king—not for the purpose of making an accusation but for the common good of the church—and having thrown himself at [the king's] feet, weeping he begged that [the king] should come at once to the aid of his desolate mother. Having called together the bishops who were there, he admonished them to go to Rome with the king and hold a synod. And it was done without delay. Now that abuser Gregory, who was seen then to be ruling the see of the Roman church, was called to the king. As he was coming to meet him—unaware of anything wrong between them, as later events showed—he met the king at Piacenza. He was honorably received, as befits a pope. Now the bishops who were there were not intending to condemn any religious bishop without trial, much less one who seemed pontiff of so great a see, and so they proceeded along together until they came to Sutri. Having arrived at that place and thinking it then proper, the king asked the pope to convene a synod. He agreed and signed the decree, for he was an uneducated man and extraordinarily simple. The synod having convened, he sat in the place of the Roman pontiff and at his order the patriarchs, metropolitans, and bishops took their seats. Among those present were Poppo, Patriarch of Aquileia, a very eloquent man; Bruno, Bishop of Augsburg; Rembaldus, Archbishop of Arles, and many more. The matter of that invader [of the Holy

See] Silvester having come up first, it was decided unanimously that he should be deprived of every episcopal and priestly office and given over to a monastery for the rest of his days. Concerning [Benedict], they judged that he ought to desist, especially since he, when he was pope, had himself foresworn the office. About the third one [Gregory himself], what were they to do? If they turned on him, accusing and testifying against the judge, he would not allow them to proceed. And so, when he was begged by the bishops [to describe] how he came to be elected, he—being uneducated—disclosed the total *puritas*[7] of the election. He declared himself to be, by the mercy of God, a priest of good witness and reputation and said that from his youth he had always cultivated bodily chastity. [He reported] that he was held by the Romans at that time to be not just praiseworthy, but nearly angelic. Because of this, he said that he had acquired much wealth, which he used in order to restore the roofs of churches and to accomplish new and bigger things in the city of Rome. And most frequently, when he was dealing with the despotism of the nobles, and how they were making popes without the election of clergy or people, he could think of nothing better to do with his wealth than to restore this right of election by clergy and people that had been unjustly suppressed by their despotism. Indeed, since his listeners were religious men, they began with great reverence to suggest to him that the skillful machinations of the ancient enemy might be at work, saying that nothing holy ought to be bought. Having been duped by these and other admonitions, he began already to conjure up in his mind the Holy Spirit and the zeal of God, whom he had experienced not according to reason. Understanding, that one addressed the bishops with these words: "I invoke God as my witness, that in my soul, oh brothers, I believed myself to be free from sin in this matter and to have been promoted to the grace [of this dignity] by God. But because now I know the tricks of the ancient enemy, you consider for the common good what ought to be done with me." To which, they responded, saying: "You consider your case in your heart, you judge yourself with your own mouth. For it is better for you to live as a poor man here with blessed Peter, for whose love you did this, in order that you may be a rich man in eternity, rather than to be resplendent in riches now and perish in eternity with Simon Magus who deceived you." Having heard this, he pronounced sentence on himself, saying "I, Bishop Gregory, servant of the servants of God, because of the most disgraceful venality of the simoniacal heresy, which the trickery of the ancient enemy insinuated into my

[7]A pun: *Puritas* can mean either purity or purulence (filled with pus).

election, I judge myself removed from the Roman See." Then he added, "Does this please you?" And they responded, "What pleases you, we confirm." The synod having been celebrated according to the rules of ecclesiastical discipline, they went to Rome greatly agitated in their minds, the king as well as the bishops, [having to confront two problems.] [First,] they had no pope who might grant the king imperial power. [Second,] in order to elect another, the clergy holding the election needed the approval of the people afterwards, but the aforesaid John [Pope Gregory who had just resigned] . . . had gotten the people to swear never to acclaim another pope while he was still alive.

In the meantime, since they could not have anyone from that very diocese [of Rome] — since, as I mentioned earlier, . . . it was impossible to find a candidate who was not illiterate, or guilty either of simony or concubinage — out of necessity they elected one of their own, Bishop Suidger of Bamberg, although the canons forbid anyone to ascend to the Roman see without having been ordained a priest or deacon in that church. Few lay persons, except those who had not sworn to John, consented by acclamation. . . .

After the king was accorded the imperial dignity, having compassion for all the civil strife there, he liberated the city from the tyranny of the nobles. The fact that he did this was praiseworthy except that what was done afterwards blemished the accomplishment. For having been misled by the rumors among the people, which should never be believed in great matters, [Henry] seized the tyranny of the office of *patricius,* as if any dignity had been constituted in the lay order that may have held more privilege than the imperial majesty. But in this calamity what could be more bitter, what more cruel than for that one, who just a little earlier had punished the Tusculans for tyranny, to want to become just like those very ones he condemned? What, for example, could have moved such a man to such a great offence, except the belief that the dignity of *patricius* would allow him to select the Roman Pontiff? But what a shame! Where was the prudence of the bishops? Where was all that knowledge of the law, if they didn't share it with the lord whom they believed they were serving? Was anyone holding the imperial dignity ever allowed to intrude himself in the election of any Roman Pontiff? Will it be allowed to anyone constituted by human power? But they said, "We read that Charles the Great was designated *patricius.*" But if they were reading this, why weren't they understanding it? At the time of Charles the Great, Constantine and Irene ruled the Roman Empire. And therefore, what could have been conferred upon the most excellent king of the Franks to expand his temporal powers except to be called father and protector of the city of

Rome? Thus we read, "Charles, king of the Franks and Lombards and *patricius* of the Romans." We also read that he increased the imperial power. But after his death, his son Louis, first among kings with foreign blood, merited the imperial benediction from the Romans, and therefore, holding the highest, he did not seek further.

14

WIBERT

How Bruno of Toul Became Pope
1054?

Having taken the honor of patricius *after the Synod of Sutri, Emperor Henry III believed he had the authority to appoint popes. His attempt to exercise this power in 1048, however, met resistance even from his own kinsman, the reformer Bruno of Toul. This account of the emperor's designation of Bruno as pope is from a biography written by Wibert, a cleric of the diocese of Toul and a close friend of Bruno. It was written after Bruno's death in 1054, but Wibert quite likely was present when these events transpired.*

At the city of Worms a large gathering occurred in the presence of the glorious Roman Emperor Henry III and the rest of the bishops and nobles. In the course of this meeting, that worthy leader [Pope Damasus II] was called to Christ and, of course, without his counsel no great matter could be decided at the imperial court. Suddenly, suspecting nothing of the sort, that one [Bruno of Toul] was elected by all gathered there to take on the burden of the apostolic office. For a long time, out of humility, he tried to refuse the honor, until he was pressured more and more. Then he demanded a respite of three days to consider the matter and during this time he remained without food or water, giving himself over to fasting and prayer. And when once more he had purged himself of all resistance to obedience, in the presence

Wibert, *Vita Leonis IX,* chap. 2.2, in *Patrologia cursus completus,* Series Latina, ed. J. P. Migne, 221 vols. (Paris: Garnier, 1844–1864), 143: 486–88.

of all he voluntarily repented of his impulse to overturn the general election, as if it was some enormity of his own wickedness. Who could describe the flood of tears elicited by his public confession when everyone's emotions were aroused to such great weeping? Whence, unanimously, that holy voice resounded in the mouths of all present: God forbid that the son who prompts such weeping be undone! Seeing, therefore, that he was in no way going to be able to escape both the general will and the imperial command, thus constrained he accepted the office imposed upon him in the presence of the Roman legates, but with one condition: that he hear through the acclamation of the entire clergy and people of Rome that they consent to this without doubt. And thus he returned to his own see, namely Toul, and celebrated the feast of our Lord's birth with great devotion in the company of four bishops—Ugo of the Italian city of Assisi, a Roman legate; Everardus archbishop of Trier; Adalbero of Metz; and Theodore bishop of Verdun. From there, guided by humility and going against all apostolic custom, he set out for Rome in the garb of a pilgrim. Tirelessly devoting himself to prayer and divine contemplation, he exerted himself out of such great solicitude not so much for the duties entrusted to him but for the care of souls. Having stopped at the city of Augsburg in the midst of this meditation, he was granted a divine consolation when he heard an angelic voice in revelation echo sweetly in harmonic melodious consonance: "The Lord said, I think thoughts of peace and not of affliction; call upon me and I will hear you, and I will lead you out of your captivity from any place." Moved by this blessed consolation, and more certain of divine help, he pushed on to complete the journey undertaken. And as was fitting for a person of such merits, he was accompanied by an infinite multitude overtaking him from all directions. Among these, a certain handmaiden of the God of religious life clung to him, and admonished him using the words of divine precept: "as soon as you shall have set foot within the doors of the church of the prince of the apostles, lest you be unmindful, use these holy words: Peace to this house (Matt. 10:12), and to all its inhabitants." He humbly accepted the command of the Lord and devoutly carried it out.

. . . Having been strengthened by the solace of the Almighty, he drew near Rome and the entire city seemed to come out to greet him with a concert of hymns. But he walked the long journey barefoot and turned his mind more to devotional thoughts than to enjoyment of the praises being sung. Who, having witnessed his contrite heart in devout prayer, who might be able to put into words, what was impenetrable even to thought, the unceasing tears descending like a stream?

Afterwards, for a long while he offered himself on the altar of his heart to Christ as "a living sacrifice, holy, and pleasing to God" (Rom. 12:1), and then he began to speak, giving a divine exhortation to the crowd of clergy and people that had flocked to him. In this brief little sermon, he made public the imperial election of himself to that difficult office and demanded urgently that they disclose their will in the matter, whatever it might be. He said that the election of the clergy and people according to the canons came before the arrangements made by others. He assured them that, unless his election were effected by the acclamation of the entire community, he would return to his country, his soul rejoicing. He revealed himself to have been forced to come to take up so great a burden. Seeing the unanimous acclamation of all, however, he continued the exhortation begun on emending one's way of life, as a suppliant asking prayers and absolution from all of them. Therefore, with the favor of divine grace and the applause of all, he was consecrated on the first Sunday of Lent, 12 February [1049], and enthroned on the apostolic throne.

15

ROMAN SYNOD

Papal Election Decree

1059

Emperor Henry III died unexpectedly after a brief illness in October 1056; his only son was six years old. Since the monarch had arranged his son's election as co-ruler and heir to the kingdom shortly after his birth, Henry IV's accession to the throne in 1056 went unchallenged. The transfer of power was well managed by Pope Victor II, who happened to have been in Germany and attended the king on his deathbed. Supposedly, the dying king committed his son to the care of the pope, who oversaw Henry IV's anointing and coronation—acts to which later reformers attributed great significance. During the young king's minority, two papal elections were held without royal consultation, but this

Kennerly M. Woody, "*Sagena piscatoris:* Peter Damiani and the Papal Election Decree of 1059," *Viator,* 1 (1970): 52–54 (Appendix: The Text of the Papal Election Decree of 1059).

changed when divisions among the reformers led to a papal schism after the death of Pope Stephen IX in Florence in March 1058. One faction in Rome elected John of Velletri as Pope Benedict X in April. Another group secured the approval of the imperial court for their choice—Gerard Bishop of Florence—and then elected him in Siena in December as Pope Nicholas II. Imperial backing, and the military support it garnered, was critical in this pope's ultimate recognition as the legitimate pontiff. Most of the leaders of important Roman churches—called "cardinals" from the Latin word cardo, *meaning "hinge" in the sense of key or central—had also backed Nicholas II. But his supporters recognized that their own ill-defined notion of free election had given Benedict X greater legitimacy than Nicholas. After all, Benedict had been elected by the clergy and the people of Rome. This decree, enacted in April 1059, served the dual purpose of legitimizing Nicholas's election (albeit after the fact) and setting forth a procedure for future papal elections. Note that it requires royal involvement. This translation follows the papal edition of the text, but significant differences in the imperial version are given in footnotes.*

In the name of the Lord God, our Savior Jesus Christ, and in the 1059th year after his incarnation during the month of April, the sacred Gospels having been brought forth, the most reverend and blessed apostolic pope Nicholas presided over a gathering of the most reverend archbishops, bishops, abbots, and venerable priests and deacons in the Constantinian basilica at the Lateran palace. And there that venerable pontiff, with apostolic authority, decreed the following concerning the election of the pope.

Your blessedness knew, dearest brothers and fellow bishops, and it did not escape the notice of lesser members [of Christ] either, that when our predecessor of pious memory Stephen died, this apostolic see, which I serve at God's command, endured so many hardships and was so exposed to those bankers of simoniacal heresy with their repeated hammering blows that, as a result, the pillar of the living God seemed about to falter and the boat of that head fisherman [Peter] forced by swelling storms down into the depths of sunken wrecks. Therefore, if it pleases you, we ought with God's help to plan prudently for future elections and provide by ecclesiastical statute for those following us, lest harmful and ineffective renovations prevail.

And therefore, instructed by the authority of our predecessors and the other holy fathers, we decree and establish: that when the pontiff of this universal Roman church dies, the cardinal bishops[8] should consult immediately among themselves and then with the cardinal clerics, diligently conferring together with due contemplation. Afterward, let the rest of the clergy and people give their assent to the new election. [We also decree] that the foremost religious men should be put forward before all the rest in the pontifical election, lest, of course, the disease of venality in any way enter into the matter. . . .

Let them elect someone from the bosom of this church, if a suitable candidate is found, or if one is not discovered from this church, a candidate from another church may be taken up. [Let them do this] without violating what is owed to the honor and reverence of our beloved son Henry, who is at present king and, God willing, in the future hopefully emperor, just as we already granted to him [through his messenger, Wibert the chancellor of Lombardy] and to his successors, who will have obtained this right personally from the apostolic see.

But if the perversity of wicked and sinful men shall have grown stronger so that a clean, honest, and free election can not be accomplished in the city of Rome, let the cardinal bishops with religious clerics and catholic lay persons, even if they are few, exercise the rightful authority[9] to elect the pontiff of the apostolic see wherever they judge more suitable.

Certainly, after the election shall have been accomplished, if a period of war or the opposition of any man in a spirit of malice shall have arisen so that he who was elected is not able to be enthroned in the apostolic see as is customary, the elect holds the same authority as the pope of ruling the holy Roman church and exercising all his powers, which we know blessed Gregory did before his consecration.

---

[8]The imperial version deletes the specification of cardinal bishops and skips to the clause preserving the emperor's rights. The deletion is significant because the cardinal priests and deacons tended to be more conservative and supportive of the tradition of imperial involvement in the Holy See. The papal version accords a leadership role to the more progressive cardinal bishops and merely a consultative role for the other cardinals.

[9]The imperial version reads ". . . and free election can not be accomplished in the city of Rome, let however few there may be exercise the rightful authority . . . ," deleting the specification of the cardinal bishops with religious clergy and catholic laypeople.

2

The Investiture Conflict

By the 1070s, efforts at reform had been underway for several decades. The importance of bishops in the process was becoming very clear. In dioceses where bishops pushed hard for change—founding new institutions to support a communal life for the clergy, weeding out married priests, visiting parishes, and attending synods—progress was being made. But in dioceses where bishops took a more gradual approach—for example, avoiding confrontations with married priests—many saw no evidence of reform. The focus of reformers at Rome, therefore, began to center on control of the episcopate, which meant control of episcopal appointments. The issue brought the papacy into direct conflict with temporal rulers. The importance of bishops as local representatives of royal power and collaborators in governance was so great that monarchs wanted only men of proven loyalty, men whom they could trust, in these positions. The idea of local communities electing such important officials seemed to be an invitation to rebellious subjects to oppose royal authority. From the papal perspective, however, thousands of souls were daily endangered by the delay of reforms, and royal appointees were more eager to serve the king than to discipline their clergy. This issue of control over bishops led to the dramatic conflict between Pope Gregory VII and Emperor Henry IV, and the struggle they initiated outlived both of them. Their successors ultimately sought concord through negotiation, but Gregory and Henry saw no room for compromise.

The Combatants:
Emperor Henry IV and Pope Gregory VII

16

An Account of Henry's Minority
ca. 1106

This highly sympathetic account of Henry IV's life, probably written just after his death in 1106, sketches the difficult youth of the boy-king. During this period, the young monarch was fought over by factions competing for power, and those who gained control of him enriched themselves at the expense of the crown. When Henry came of age in 1065 (he was fifteen), he distanced himself from these counselors and set about the difficult work of rebuilding royal power. The experiences of his youth, however, made him extremely sensitive throughout his adult life about any challenge to his royal prerogatives.

When Emperor Henry whom we discuss here, still a boy, succeeded in the kingship his father, the most glorious Emperor Henry III (for while he was still a boy his father yielded to nature), war did not disturb the peace; trumpet calls did not break the quiet; rapine was not rampant; fidelity did not speak falsely—since the kingdom yet held to its former state. Justice was still full of its own vigor; power was still full of its own right. Agnes, the most serene Empress, a woman of manly disposition, sustained greatly this happy state of the kingdom, she who together with her son with equal right governed the commonwealth. But since immature age inspires too little fear, and while awe languishes, audacity increases, the boyish years of the King excited in many the spirit of crime. Therefore, everyone strove to become equal to the one greater than him, or even greater, and the

---

Vita Heinrici IV imperatoris, chap. 2, in *Imperial Lives and Letters of the Eleventh Century,* trans. Theodor E. Mommsen and Karl F. Morrison (New York: Columbia University Press, 1962; rpt. 2000), 105–7.

might of many increased through crime; nor was there any fear of the law, which had little authority under the boy-king.

And so that they could do everything with more license, they first robbed of her child the mother whose mature wisdom and grave habits they feared, pleading that it was dishonorable for the kingdom to be administered by a woman (although one may read of many queens who administered kingdoms with manly wisdom).[1] But after the boy-king, once drawn away from the bosom of his mother, came into the hands of the princes to be raised, whatever they prescribed for him to do, he did like the boy he was. Whomever they wished, he exalted; whomever they wished, he set down; so that they may rightly be said not to have ministered (*ministrasse*) to their king so much as to have given orders (*imperasse*) to him. When they dealt with the affairs of the kingdom, they took counsel not so much for the affairs of the kingdom as for their own; and in everything they did, it was their primary concern to put their own advantage above everything else.

This was certainly the greatest perfidy, that they left to his own devices in his boyish acts him who ought to have been kept, so to speak, under seal, in order thus to elicit from him what they strove to obtain.

But when he passed into that measure of age and mind in which he could discern what was honorable, what shameful, what useful, and what was not, he reconsidered what he had done while led by the suggestion of the princes and condemned many things which he had done. And, having become his own judge, he changed those of his acts which were to be changed. He also prohibited wars, violence, and rapine; he strove to recall peace and justice, which had been expelled, to restore neglected laws, and to check the license of crime. Those accustomed to crime whom he could not coerce by edict, he corrected, more mildly, indeed, than the wrong demanded by the stricture of the law and the legal prerogative of the court. Those men called this not justice, but injury; and they who had cast law aside disdained to be bound by law, just as they who were racing through every impiety, disdained to suffer the reins, and they gave their attention to plans by which they might either kill him or deprive him of his office, not remembering that they owed peace to their citizens, justice to the kingdom, fidelity to the King.

---

[1]The author is alluding to the "Kaiserswerth coup," when in 1062 a faction led by Archbishop Anno of Cologne kidnapped Henry and took over the regency. Henry was 12 years old.

17

POPE GREGORY VII

A Letter to Supporters in Lombardy

July 1, 1073

A few weeks before he died in April 1073, Pope Alexander II had excommunicated several of Henry IV's closest advisers at a synod held in Rome. The reasons are not spelled out in the acts of the synod but probably were related to the king's support of a new archbishop, Godfrey, for the important imperial see of Milan. Godfrey was the handpicked successor of Archbishop Guido of Milan and had the support of other Lombard bishops: These parties had sought imperial approval and investiture of Godfrey. The Patarenes (Documents 6 and 7), however, charged that Godfrey was a simonist and blocked his entry into the city. This early letter of the new pope—Hildebrand, who took the name of Gregory VII—rallies reformers in northern Italy against Archbishop Godfrey, but it also reveals the worldview of its author. Born in southern Tuscany, Hildebrand was educated in Rome and entered religious life there, most likely in the monastery of St. Mary's-on-the-Aventine. He served as Pope Gregory VI's chaplain and followed him into exile in Germany, spending time at the imperial court of Henry III. Hildebrand returned to Rome in the entourage of Bruno of Toul (Pope Leo IX) and became a central figure in reforming circles. A man of passionate religious conviction, Pope Gregory VII saw the events of his time in an apocalyptic framework: Good and evil, God and Satan, were locked in combat, and the souls of all Christians were at stake.

Gregory, bishop, servant of those who serve God, to all faithful followers of St. Peter, prince of the Apostles, especially to those dwelling in Lombardy, greeting and apostolic benediction.

I desire you to know, beloved brethren, as many of you do know already, that we are so placed that, whether we will or no, we are bound to proclaim truth and righteousness to all peoples, especially to

The Correspondence of Pope Gregory VII, ed. and trans. Ephraim Emerton (New York: Columbia University Press, 1932; rpt. 1969), 11–12.

Christians, according to the word of the Lord: "Cry aloud; spare not, lift up thy voice like a trumpet and declare unto my people their transgressions!" (Isa. 58:1). And elsewhere: "If thou shalt not declare his wickedness unto the wicked, I will require his soul at thy hand" (Ezek. 3:18). Also saith the prophet: "Cursed be he that keepeth back his sword from blood!" (Jer. 48:10), that is, he that keepeth back the word of preaching from reproving the carnally minded. We make this prelude because, among the many ills which afflict the whole world, certain ministers of Satan and heralds of Antichrist in Lombardy are striving to overturn even the Christian faith and thus are bringing down the wrath of God upon themselves.

As you well know, during the life of Guido, called archbishop of Milan, Godfrey had the audacity to purchase, like any vile wench, that church which once through the merits of Mary, most glorious Virgin and Mother of God, and through the fame of that most noted doctor, St. Ambrose, shone forth among the churches of Lombardy by its piety, its freedom and its own peculiar glory—that is to say, he prostituted the bride of Christ to the Devil and befouled her with the criminal heresy of Simony by trying to separate her from the catholic faith.

Hearing of this the Roman Church, mother of you and, as you know, mistress [*magistra*] of all Christendom, called together a council from several countries and, supported by the approval of many priests and members of divers orders, through the authority of St. Peter, prince of the apostles, pierced him with the lance of anathema as an enemy of the catholic faith and of the canon law, together with all those who took his part. This right of excommunication, as even the enemies of the Church cannot deny, was approved of old by holy fathers and has been confirmed and is still confirmed by Catholics through all the holy churches.

Wherefore, beloved brethren, in the name of Almighty God, Father, Son and Holy Spirit, and of the blessed Peter and Paul, chiefs of the Apostles, we warn, exhort and command you to have no dealings whatever with the aforesaid heretic Godfrey, seeing that to side with him in this crime is to deny the faith of Christ. Resist him by whatever means you can as sons of God and defend the Christian faith whereby you are to be saved. And let no pride of men deter you; for he who is with us is greater than all, is ever unconquered, and it is his will that we labor for him, and he will give the crown to those who fight fairly, as the Apostle promises. For our captain [*dux*] is wont to crush the many and the proud by means of the few and humble, and to confound the things that are strong by the things that are weak. Such is the will and pleasure of our invincible prince.

May Almighty God, who especially entrusted his sheep to St. Peter and gave him rule over all the Church, strengthen you in your devotion to him so that, delivered from your sins by his authority, you may have grace to withstand the enemies of God and win their hearts to repentence.

18

POPE GREGORY VII

A Letter to Duke Rudolf of Swabia concerning Henry IV

September 1, 1073

Gregory's ideas about papal authority developed over the course of his stormy pontificate, and this early letter reveals a traditional, Gelasian understanding of the relationship between regnum *(temporal authority) and* sacerdotium *(spiritual authority). It also indicates that Gregory was present at the imperial court when Henry III had his infant son elected as co-ruler and believed that he had some special responsibility to counsel the monarch. The closing lines of the letter reveal how Gregory identified himself with Saint Peter, a trait even more prominent in subsequent correspondence (see Document 20). The recipient of this letter would be elected antiking in 1077.*

Gregory . . . to Rudolf, duke of Swabia, greeting. . . .

Although your zeal in the past has made it clear that you are devoted to the honor of the Holy Roman Church, your recent letter shows your fervent affection for it and proves how greatly you surpass

The Correspondence of Pope Gregory VII, ed. and trans. Ephraim Emerton (New York: Columbia University Press, 1932; rpt. 1969), 15–16.

all the other princes of those parts in this respect. Among other welcome expressions therein, this seemed especially calculated to advance the glory of the imperial government and also to strengthen the power of Holy Church, namely, that the empire and the priesthood should be bound together in harmonious union. For as the human body is guided by two eyes for its physical illumination, so the body of the Church is guided and enlightened with spiritual light when these two offices work together in the cause of pure religion.

Wherefore we desire Your Excellency to know that we have no ill will toward King Henry, to whom we are under obligation because he was our choice as king, and because his father of honored memory, the emperor Henry, treated me with especial honor among all the Italians at his court, and at his death commended his son to the Roman Church in the person of Pope Victor [II] of reverend memory. Nor, so God help us, would we willingly hate any Christian man, according to the word of the Apostle: "If I give my body to be burned, and if I bestow all my goods to feed the poor and have not love, I am nothing" (1 Cor. 13:3). But, since the harmony of Empire and Priesthood ought to be pure and free from all deceit, it seems to us highly important first to take counsel with you and the empress Agnes, the countess Beatrice, and Rainald, bishop of Como, and other God-fearing men. Then, after you have thoroughly understood our wishes, if our reasons seem sound to you, you may come to an agreement with us; but, if you find that anything should be added to our arguments or stricken from them, we shall be ready, with God's approval, to accept your advice.

Wherefore we urge you to strive ever more earnestly to increase your loyalty to St. Peter and to come without delay to his shrine, both to offer your prayers and for the sake of the great advantage it may bring. You will place St. Peter on both accounts so greatly in debt to you that you will enjoy his intercession both in this life and in the life to come.

19

POPE GREGORY VII

The Dictatus papae

1075

This list of twenty-seven assertions about papal authority appears in the register of Gregory's letters between documents dated March 3 and 5, 1075. Given the unquestioned authenticity of this register, the list was almost certainly dictated by the pope. These claims were not, however, distributed or circulated. There are no direct references to them in Gregory's correspondence or in the polemical writings of the late eleventh century. Even in canon law collections of the period they are only rarely cited. What was their purpose? H. E. J. Cowdrey has called attention to a statement of Peter Damian in a 1059 letter that Hildebrand/Gregory had asked him to compile papal decrees and statements on the authority of the Apostolic See and suggested that this list was Gregory's own draft of propositions on papal prerogatives. They may well have been prepared with the expectation that Henry IV would soon come to Rome to be crowned emperor. In exchange for his coronation, Henry would have been required to acknowledge the rights of the Roman Church. This scenario never developed, but the Dictatus papae *gives us valuable evidence of Gregory's conception of his office on the eve of his bitter struggle with Henry IV.*

I. That the Roman Church was founded by God alone.

II. That only the Roman Pontiff may by right be called universal.

III. That he alone can depose or restore bishops.

IV. That his legate takes precedence in council before all bishops, even if he is of a lower rank, and has the power to pass a sentence of deposition against them.

V. That the pope may depose the absent.

VI. That, among other things, we ought not stay in the same house with those excommunicated by him.

Das Register Gregors VII, 2.55a, ed. E. Caspar, in *Monumenta Germaniae historica, Epistolae Selectae,* 2 (Berlin: Wiedmann, 1920), 201–8.

VII. That only he may establish new laws as necessary, may form new parishes, may make an abbey of a canonry (and the contrary), and may divide rich dioceses and unite impoverished ones.

VIII. That only he may use imperial insignia.

IX. That all princes should kiss the feet of the pope alone.

X. That his name alone may be read out in churches.

XI. That this title [pope] is unique in the world.

XII. That he may depose emperors.

XIII. That he may transfer bishops from see to see as he thinks necessary.

XIV. That he may ordain a cleric from any church to wherever he wishes.

XV. That someone having been ordained by him may rule over another church, but not under the command of others, and that he ought not to accept a higher rank from any other bishop.

XVI. That no synod ought to be called general [meaning universal] without his mandate.

XVII. That no chapter or book may be regarded as canonical without his authority.

XVIII. That no ruling of his may be retracted by anyone and that he alone of all men may retract [a sentence he has given].

XIX. That he may be judged by no one.

XX. That none should dare to condemn someone appealing to the Apostolic See.

XXI. That major cases of any church whatsoever should be referred to him.

XXII. That the Roman Church has never erred, nor will it ever err, as scripture attests.

XXIII. That the Roman Pontiff, if he shall have been canonically ordained, is undoubtedly made holy by the merits of blessed Peter, as Saint Ennodius Bishop of Pavia attests, with many holy fathers supporting him, and as is contained in the decrees of blessed Pope Symmachus.[2]

XXIV. That by his order and license subordinate persons may bring accusations.

XXV. That he may depose or reinstate bishops without calling a synod.

---

[2]Ennodius of Pavia wrote a tract in 502 defending Pope Symmachus (498–514) from accusations of immorality; it asserted that popes could only be judged by God. An early collection of decrees supporting papal authority was attributed to Pope Symmachus.

XXVI. That someone not in concord with the Roman Church may not be held to be Catholic.

XXVII. That he may absolve subjects from fealty to unjust men.

The First Confrontation

20

POPE GREGORY VII

Admonition to Henry

December 8, 1075

When things were going badly in the Saxon war, Henry had adopted a conciliatory posture with Gregory. The pope probably considered this a favorable sign that a penitent and pliant king would soon come to Rome to be instructed by the Holy See before coronation. All this changed in the summer of 1075 when Henry won a resounding military victory over the Saxon rebels at Homburg on June 9. Now in a position of strength, he resumed his campaign to restore royal authority. While he had been battling the Saxon rebels, events in Milan had changed rapidly in his favor. During Holy Week of 1075 the Patarenes precipitated a new wave of violence; this time they were defeated. Henry took the opportunity to appoint another imperial candidate as archbishop, a local Milanese cleric named Tedald. In doing so, he disregarded entirely the claims not only of the papal candidate to the see, Atto, but also those of his own earlier candidate, Godfrey. Henry also invested new bishops for two other Italian sees, Fermo and Spoleto. It is important to note at this junction that in these investitures Henry was acting entirely within his rights. Historians once believed there was a papal decree against lay investiture enacted at the Roman synod of 1075, but no such canon survives, and none of the documentation of the period clarifies the issue. Indeed, Gregory's objection to Henry's actions concerning Fermo and Spoleto had nothing to do with investiture: It was because the candidates were strangers to

The Correspondence of Pope Gregory VII, ed. and trans. Ephraim Emerton (New York: Columbia University Press, 1932; rpt. 1969), 86–90.

him. It seems likely, however, that a proclamation against lay investiture was discussed at the 1075 synod but never promulgated. Some evidence of this lies in a number of ongoing disputes Gregory had with leading German prelates over their treatment of monastic institutions and accusations of simony. Gregory apparently felt there was little hope of reforming the church in the German lands if he could not exert greater control over the bishops there. This letter has sometimes been described as a papal "ultimatum," but there are numerous conciliatory clauses amidst Gregory's usual righteous rhetoric. There is no doubt, however, that the verbal admonitions the pope sent through the three legates mentioned at the letter's close were much more stern. They very likely made a blunt connection between full compliance with papal demands and imperial coronation, as well as spelling out the consequences—including excommunication and deposition—of continued disobedience.

Gregory, bishop, servant of God's servants, to King Henry, greeting and the apostolic benediction—but with the understanding that he obeys the Apostolic See as becomes a Christian king.

Considering and weighing carefully to how strict a judge we must render any account of the stewardship committed to us by St. Peter, prince of the Apostles, we have hesitated to send you the apostolic benediction, since you are reported to be in voluntary communication with men who are under the censure of the Apostolic See and of a synod. If this is true, you yourself know that you cannot receive the favor of God nor the apostolic blessing unless you shall first put away those excommunicated persons and force them to do penance and shall yourself obtain absolution and forgiveness for your sin by due repentance and satisfaction. Wherefore we counsel Your Excellency, if you feel yourself guilty in this matter, to make your confession at once to some pious bishop who, with our sanction, may impose upon you a penance suited to the offense, may absolve you and with your consent in writing may be free to send us a true report of the manner of your penance.

We marvel exceedingly that you have sent us so many devoted letters and displayed such humility by the spoken words of your legates, calling yourself a son of our Holy Mother Church and subject to us in the faith, singular in affection, a leader in devotion, commending yourself with every expression of gentleness and reverence, and yet in action showing yourself most bitterly hostile to the canons and apostolic decrees in those duties especially required by loyalty to the Church. Not to mention other cases, the way you have observed your promises in the Milan affair, made through your mother and through bishops, our colleagues, whom we sent to you, and what your intentions were in making them is evident to all. And now, heaping wounds upon wounds, you have handed over the sees of Fermo and Spoleto — if indeed a church may be given over by any human power — to persons entirely unknown to us, whereas it is not lawful to consecrate anyone except after probation and with due knowledge.

It would have been becoming to you, since you confess yourself to be a son of the Church, to give more respectful attention to the master of the Church, that is, to Peter, prince of the Apostles. To him, if you are of the Lord's flock, you have been committed for your pasture, since Christ said to him: "Peter, feed my sheep" (John 21:17), and again: "to thee are given the keys of Heaven, and whatsoever thou shalt bind on earth shall be bound in Heaven and whatsoever thou shalt loose on earth shall be loosed in Heaven" (Matt. 16:19). Now, while we, unworthy sinner that we are, stand in his place of power, still whatever you send to us, whether in writing or by word of mouth, he himself receives, and while we read what is written or hear the voice of those who speak, he discerns with subtle insight from what spirit the message comes. Wherefore Your Highness should beware lest any defect of will toward the Apostolic See be found in your words or in your messages and should pay due reverence, not to us but to Almighty God, in all matters touching the welfare of the Christian faith and the status of the Church. And this we say although our Lord deigned to declare: "He who heareth you heareth me; and he who despiseth you despiseth me" (Luke 10:16).

We know that one who does not refuse to obey God in those matters in which we have spoken according to the statutes of the holy fathers does not scorn to observe our admonitions even as if he had received them from the lips of the Apostle himself. For if our Lord, out of reverence for the chair of Moses, commanded the Apostles to observe the teaching of the scribes and pharisees who sat thereon, there can be no doubt that the apostolic and gospel teaching, whose seat and foundation is Christ, should be accepted and maintained by those who are chosen to the service of teaching.

At a synod held at Rome during the current year, and over which Divine Providence willed us to preside, several of your subjects being present, we saw that the order of the Christian religion had long been greatly disturbed and its chief and proper function, the redemption of

souls, had fallen low and through the wiles of the Devil had been trodden under foot. Startled by this danger and by the manifest ruin of the
Lord's flock we returned to the teaching of the holy fathers, declaring
no novelties nor any inventions of our own, but holding that the primary and only rule of discipline and the well-trodden way of the saints
should again be sought and followed, all wandering paths to be abandoned. For we know that there is no other way of salvation and eternal
life for the flock of Christ and their shepherds except that shown by
him who said: "I am the door and he who enters by me shall be saved
and shall find pasture." This was taught by the Apostles and observed
by the holy fathers and we have learned it from the Gospels and from
every page of Holy Writ.

This edict,[3] which some who place the honor of men above that of
God call an intolerable burden, we, using the right word, call rather a
truth and a light necessary for salvation, and we have given judgment
that it is to be heartily accepted and obeyed, not only by you and your
subjects but by all princes and peoples who confess and worship
Christ—though it is our especial wish and would be especially fitting
for you, that you should excel others in devotion to Christ as you are
their superior in fame, in station and in valor.

Nevertheless, in order that these demands may not seem to you
too burdensome or unfair we have sent you word by your own liege-
men not to be troubled by this reform of an evil practice but to send
us prudent and pious legates from your own people. If these can show
in any reasonable way how we can moderate the decision of the holy
fathers saving the honor of the eternal king and without peril to our
own soul, we will condescend to hear their counsel. It would in fact
have been the fair thing for you, even if you had not been so graciously admonished, to make reasonable inquiry of us in what respect
we had offended you or assailed your honor, before you proceeded to
violate the apostolic decrees. But how little you cared for our warnings
or for doing right was shown by your later actions.

However, since the long-enduring patience of God summons you to
improvement, we hope that with increase of understanding your heart
and mind may be turned to obey the commands of God. We warn you
with a father's love that you accept the rule of Christ, that you consider the peril of preferring your own honor to his, that you do not
hamper by your actions the freedom of that church which he deigned
to bind to himself as a bride by a divine union, but, that she may

---

[3]What "edict" this is remains unclear. Scholars once thought it referred to an edict
against investiture, but the evidence for such a decree this early is weak.

increase as greatly as possible, you will begin to lend to Almighty God and to St. Peter, by whom also your own glory may merit increase, the aid of your valor by faithful devotion.

Now you ought to recognize your special obligation to them for the triumph over your enemies which they have granted you, and while they are making you happy and singularly prosperous, they ought to find your devotion increased by their favor to you. That the fear of God, in whose hand is all the might of kings and emperors, may impress this upon you more than any admonitions of mine, bear in mind what happened to Saul after he had won a victory by command of the prophet, how he boasted of his triumph, scorning the prophet's admonitions, and how he was rebuked by the Lord, and also what favor followed David the king as a reward for his humility in the midst of the tokens of his bravery.

Finally, as to what we have read in your letters and do not mention here we will give you no decided answer until your legates, Radbod, Adalbert and Odescalcus, to whom we entrust this, have returned to us and have more fully reported your decision upon the matters which we commissioned them to discuss with you.

21

EMPEROR HENRY IV

Response to Gregory's Admonition
Early 1076

The twenty-five-year-old king was at Goslar celebrating the Christmas holidays when Gregory's "admonition" arrived. His anger was evident in his immediate responses. He publicly consorted with those excommunicated counselors whom the pope had forbidden him to see, and he called an assembly of bishops and lay princes to convene at Worms in January. Although the number of lay leaders in attendance was low, a large majority of the bishops of the realm came to Worms. They renounced their allegiance to Gregory as pope, declaring him an arrogant usurper

Imperial Lives and Letters of the Eleventh Century, trans. Theodor E. Mommsen and Karl F. Morrison (New York: Columbia University Press, 1962; rpt. 2000), 150–51.

of the Holy See. These two letters had two very different audiences. Henry sent the first to Gregory with a copy of the Worms renunciation. The second letter he circulated in Germany to cultivate support for his actions. He refers several times to Gregory's proclivity—in Milan through his support of the Pataria and in several German sees—to call upon the common people to disobey ecclesiastical lords whom the pope opposed.

Henry, King by the grace of God, to Hildebrand:

Although hitherto I hoped for those things from you which are expected of a father and obeyed you in all respects to the great indignation of our vassals, I have obtained from you a requital suitable from one who was the most pernicious enemy of our life and kingly office. After you had first snatched away with arrogant boldness all the hereditary dignity owed me by that [Apostolic] See, going still further you tried with the most evil arts to alienate the kingdom of Italy. Not content with this, you have not feared to set your hand against the most reverend bishops, who are united to us like most cherished members and have harassed them with most arrogant affronts and the bitterest abuses against divine and human laws. While I let all these things go unnoticed through patience, you thought it not patience but cowardice and dared to rise up against the head itself, announcing, as you know, that (to use your own words) you would either die or deprive me of my life and kingly office.

Judging that this unheard of defiance had to be confuted not with words, but with action, I held a general assembly of all the foremost men of their kingdom, at their supplication. When they had made public through their true declaration (which you will hear from their own letter) those things they had previously kept silent through fear and reverence, they took public action to the end that you could no longer continue in the Apostolic See. Since their sentence seemed just and righteous before God and men, I also give my assent, revoking from you every prerogative of the papacy which you have seemed to hold, and ordering [you] to descend from the throne of the city whose patriciate is due me through the bestowal of God and the sworn assent of the Romans.

[Propaganda Version]

Henry, King not by usurpation, but by the pious ordination of God, to Hildebrand, now not Pope, but false monk:

You have deserved such a salutation as this because of the confusion you have wrought; for you left untouched no order of the Church which you could make a sharer of confusion instead of honor, of malediction instead of benediction.

For to discuss a few outstanding points among many: Not only have you dared to touch the rectors of the holy Church—the archbishops, the bishops, and the priests, anointed of the Lord as they are—but you have trodden them under foot like slaves who know not what their lord may do. In crushing them you have gained for yourself acclaim from the mouth of the rabble. You have judged that all these know nothing, while you alone know everything. In any case, you have sedulously used this knowledge not for edification, but for destruction, so greatly that we may believe Saint Gregory, whose name you have arrogated to yourself, rightly made this prophesy of you when he said: "From the abundance of his subjects, the mind of the prelate is often exalted, and he thinks that he has more knowledge than anyone else, since he sees that he has more power than anyone else."

And we, indeed, bore with all these abuses, since we were eager to preserve the honor of the Apostolic See. But you construed our humility as fear, and so you were emboldened to rise up even against the royal power itself, granted to us by God. You dared to threaten to take the kingship away from us—as though we had received the kingship from you, as though kingship and empire were in your hand and not in the hand of God.

Our Lord, Jesus Christ, has called us to kingship, but has not called you to the priesthood. For you have risen by these steps: namely, by cunning, which the monastic profession abhors, to money; by money to favor; by favor to the sword. By the sword you have come to the throne of peace, and from the throne of peace you have destroyed the peace. You have armed subjects against their prelates; you who have not been called by God have taught that our bishops who have been called by God are to be spurned; you have usurped for laymen the bishops' ministry over priests, with the result that these laymen depose and condemn the very men whom the laymen themselves received as teachers from the hand of God, through the imposition of the hands of bishops.

You have also touched me, one who, though unworthy, has been anointed to kingship among the anointed. This wrong you have done to me, although as the tradition of the holy Fathers has taught, I am to be judged by God alone and am not to be deposed for any crime unless—may it never happen—I should deviate from the Faith. For the prudence of the holy bishops entrusted the judgment and the deposition even of [the late Roman emperor] Julian the Apostate not to themselves, but to God alone. The true pope Saint Peter also exclaims, "Fear God, honor the king." You, however, since you do not fear God, dishonor me, ordained of Him.

Wherefore, when Saint Paul gave no quarter to an angel from heaven if the angel should preach heterodoxy, he did not except you who are now teaching heterodoxy throughout the earth. For he says, "If anyone, either I or an angel from heaven, preach any other gospel unto you than that which we have preached unto you, let him be accursed." Descend, therefore, condemned by this anathema and by the common judgment of all our bishops and of ourself. Relinquish the Apostolic See which you have arrogated. Let another mount the throne of Saint Peter, another who will not cloak violence with religion but who will teach the pure doctrine of Saint Peter.

I, Henry, King by the grace of God, together with all our bishops say to you: Descend! Descend!

Canossa

22

LAMPERT OF HERSFELD

Account of Canossa

ca. 1077

Gregory's response to Henry was equally decisive. At the Roman Lenten synod of 1076 (February 14–20), he excommunicated the king, declared him deposed, released his subjects and vassals from their sworn allegiance — tantamount to urging them to rebel — and forbade anyone to serve Henry as king. Divine censure seemed to follow papal condemnation: After the monarch held a crown-wearing ceremony in the Utrecht

Lampert of Hersfeld, *Annales,* ed. O. Holder-Egger, in *Monumenta Germaniae historica, Scriptores rerum Germanicarum in usum scholarum,* 38 (Hannover: Hahn, 1894), 283–84, 285–98.

cathedral on Easter Sunday, the church was struck by lightning and burned to the ground. Henry's support deteriorated precipitously, a key blow being Bishop Hermann of Metz's release of the prisoners from the Saxon war. By summer Saxony was in open revolt again, and Henry's attempts to put down the uprising were ineffectual. In September, Gregory corresponded with Henry's opponents and broached the subject of electing a new king. An assembly of princes in October attended by papal legates forced Henry to promise obedience to the pope and to agree to an assembly in Augsburg on February 2, 1077, where Gregory himself would resolve the matter of the kingship. Henry did not want to give his enemies such an opportunity. This account of what Henry did between December 1076 and January 1077 was written by a monk named Lampert at the imperial abbey of Hersfeld. Although his monastery remained loyal to Henry IV and was visited several times by the emperor, Lampert had greater sympathy for Henry's Saxon opponents.

The king, however, knew that his safety depended entirely on that one [the pope] if he were to be absolved from the excommunication by the anniversary day. By his own calculation, he thought it not safe enough—with the arrival of the pontiff expected in Gaul—to have his case heard either by that aggressive judge or by his determined accusers. He judged it best for himself instead, given the way things stood, that he hurry to intercept the Roman pontiff in Italy as he was setting out for Germany and attempt to obtain absolution from the excommunication in any way he could. That accomplished, no matters of conscience would prevent the easy resolution of the rest of his difficulties through discussion with the princes, taking counsel and asking the help of loyal friends in adversity.

Therefore, leaving Speyer a few days before Christmas with his wife and infant son, the journey was begun. That noble man left the realm accompanied by not a soul from Germany save one notable neither for his lineage nor his wealth. Since he needed resources for so long a journey, Henry sought aid from many men he had often benefitted when his kingdom was intact. There were very few, however, who relieved his necessity to any extent, moved either by memory of past favors or by the present spectacle of human events. And thus the king descended suddenly from the height of glory and greatest wealth to such distress and calamity! Similarly, the other excommunicates,[4]

---

[4]*the other excommunicates:* These were five of Henry's closest advisers.

eager to obtain absolution more quickly, very eagerly hurried along to Italy. But they agreed not to allow the king into their traveling company, deterred by fear of the princes or even the Roman pontiff. . . .

Setting out for Italy King Henry celebrated Christmas in Burgundy in the place called Besançon, having been received rather splendidly, considering the straits he was in. He stayed with Count William, his mother's uncle, whose resources were most ample and flourishing in these regions. His situation next was this: he had already left the direct route in Burgundy, because he had certain knowledge that Dukes Rudolf, Welf, and Berthold had expected him and had placed guards on all the roads and passes (vulgarly called "clusas") that lead into Italy so that no means of access would be afforded him there. Setting out again after the observance of Christmas, when he had come to the place called Civis[5] he met his mother-in-law and her son, named Amedeo, whose authority in these regions was very great, their possessions most ample and name quite celebrated. They received his coming honorably. All the same, they did not want to concede passage to him through their borders unless he handed over five Italian sees bordering their possessions. To all the counselors of the king, this seemed too harsh and intolerable. But necessity inevitably laid heavy upon him and here was a way he could buy his route. Since these two were moved neither by rights of kinship nor by pity at so great a calamity, much effort and time having already been consumed in this deliberation, it was only just barely managed that his relations deigned to accept a certain well-endowed province of Burgundy as the price of allowing transit. The Lord's indignation had turned away from Henry not only those obliged to him through oaths and frequent benefits, but even friends and close relatives.

Passage having been obtained with such great difficulty, immediately another difficulty followed on its heels. The winter was extremely bitter and the range of mountains they traveled through—vast in extent, with their summits pressing nearly through the clouds—were so stiffened with great snow drifts and icy cold temperatures that the steps of neither horses nor foot-travelers were without danger in the slippery and precipitous descents. But with the anniversary day of the king's excommunication drawing near, he allowed no slackening of the journey because unless he was absolved from excommunication by that day, he knew that it would be decreed with the general consensus of

[5]*Civis:* Probably Gex, near Geneva.

the princes that his cause would have been lost forever and that he would have lost his kingdom without any hope of its restitution.[6] Therefore, he hired experienced locals accustomed to scaling the steep summits of the Alps. These [men] went before through the snowpack and relieved however they could the difficulty of those following. Even with these guides, when they with great difficulty climbed to the top of Mont-Cenis, there was no way of making further progress, [so steep was the mountain side] and, as stated above, so utterly treacherous with glacial ice, that it seemed to deny any descent. There the men attempting with all their strength to avoid danger were reduced to creeping along on their hands and feet or leaning on the arms of the guides while staggering, their steps slipping on the ice and floundering at length, so that they arrived at the plain at last with their health gravely compromised. The hired guides drew down the queen, and other women who were in her entourage, lying in ox hides. They lowered some horses via certain contraptions and others they dragged with their feet tied together. Many of these horses died while being pulled and others were crippled; few were able to avoid danger, all in one piece and unhurt.

Rumors spread through Italy that the king had come and that he had already overcome the harsh mountains to enter Italy. All the bishops and counts of Italy flocked to him eagerly and received him with great honor worthy of his royal magnificence. Within a few days an army of infinite multitudes had gathered about him. There were those who from the beginning of his reign had wanted him to enter Italy because that kingdom was besieged with wars, sedition, brigandage, and other various disturbances. Now they hoped that royal severity would correct all those presumptuous acts of wicked men that were contrary to the law and the rights of the majority. Moreover, because the rumor had spread that Henry was hastening with a bellicose passion to depose the pope, they rejoiced at the opportunity offered to suitably avenge wrongs done to them by that [man, Gregory,] who long ago had suspended them from ecclesiastical communion.[7]

Meanwhile, by letter the pope had called the German princes (who

[6]Lampert is here voicing the position of those who were intent on deposing Henry. The majority of the German princes, however, took the more moderate position that Henry, even if he was found guilty by the pope at the Augsburg assembly, could be absolved from the excommunication and restored to the kingship then.

[7]Gregory had excommunicated all the bishops of Lombardy supporting Henry at the Lenten synod of 1076.

had gathered at Oppenheim) to convene at Augsburg on the feast of the Purification of the Virgin [February 2] to discuss the case of the king. The Roman princes were reluctant and opposed his undertaking the journey because of the uncertain outcome of the venture. Still the pope left Rome, hurrying as much as possible, since he was hard pressed to reach Augsburg by the appointed day. Mathilda [Countess of Tuscany], the abandoned wife of Duke Gozelo [Goffredo the Hunchback] of Lotharingia and daughter of Marquis Boniface, and the Countess Beatrice offered him safe-conduct. This woman, when her husband was still alive, gave the impression of being a widow, spending long periods apart from him. When she had not wanted to follow her husband away from her native land to Lotharingia, he—who was charged with administering Lotharingia and tied up with matters there—only rarely visited the March of Italy after three or four years. After his death [February 27, 1076], she stayed with the Roman pontiff nearly like an inseparable partner and she cherished him with great affection. Since a great part of Italy obeyed her authority and she was richer than any other prince of that land in all things over which mortals first held sway, wherever the pope had needed of her help, she was at hand and gave diligent service as to a father or lord. As a result, in the gossip even among the king's supporters — especially the clerics, to whom any illicit marriage contracted against the canons was prohibited [by this same pope] — he was not able to avoid suspicion of an unholy love. The talk had the pope night and day shamelessly rolling about in Mathilda's arms and speculated that [this] preoccupation with these furtive papal trysts kept her from contracting another marriage after the death of her spouse. But among persons with any sense, it was clearly recognized that all this talk was false. For the pope had established such a distinguished and apostolic way of life that the sublimity of his conduct admitted not the least stain of evil rumor and she, so well known in Rome and in such frequent sight of observers, would never have been able to hide the perpetration of something obscene. Indeed the signs and portents, which became more frequent through the prayers of the pope, and his most fervent zeal for God and for ecclesiastical law strengthened him enough against the poisonous tongues of his detractors. The pope therefore, while he hastened toward Gaul, heard unexpectedly that the king was already in Italy. At the encouragement of Mathilda, he turned aside to a very fortified castle called Canossa, wanting to wait until he might investigate more diligently the purpose of Henry's coming, namely whether he came to apply for pardon or instead, enraged and ready to take revenge with military force for the injury of his excommunication. . . .

The rest of the bishops and laymen whom the pope had excommunicated (and whom the king for this reason had removed from his side, constrained as he was by extreme necessity) arrived in Italy safely having eluded those holding the passes against them. And finding the pope at Canossa, they sought pardon for their supposed rebellion supplicating him with bare feet and wearing penitential woolens in order that they might be absolved from the excommunication. To those who truly acknowledged and bewailed their sin, Gregory did not deny mercy. But he said that their long disobedience and the deeply encrusted rust of sin ought to be burned up and boiled away by daily penance. If, in fact, they were truly penitent they would bear whatever branding iron of ecclesiastical chastisement he might use to heal the wounds of ecclesiastical corruption, lest the hideous and violent fault perpetrated against the apostolic see might, through ease of pardon, seem either small or nothing at all. To these declaring themselves ready for all the privation which he would impose, Gregory ordered each of the bishops to be enclosed alone in individual cells, not to have any conversation with anyone, and to receive a small measure of food and drink in the evening. He ordered a penance for each layman that took into consideration the age and strength of each. After some days he finally called the prostrate to him and when he had mildly rebuked them for the crimes committed and warned them never to do anything like it again, he absolved them from excommunication. As they departed, he ordered that above all, repeating again and again, they must not associate to any extent with King Henry until he had made satisfaction for the injury done to the Holy See. Nor [might they] assist him in any way in overthrowing the present public order or destroy the peace of the church. They were all, however, allowed to talk to him for one purpose: in order to incite him to penance and to be turned aside from the path of evil works on which he seemed to be careening headlong.

Meanwhile, King Henry summoned Countess Mathilda to speak with him and sent her loaded down with pleas and promises for the pope, along with her mother-in-law and her son, Marquis Azzo, the abbot of Cluny, and others from among the Italian princes whose authority was not in doubt with him [the pope]. He pleaded to be absolved from the excommunication and that blind faith not be accorded the German princes who had been stirred up to accuse him, stimulated more by envy than by zeal for justice. The pope, having heard this embassy, said that it would be entirely improper and unheard of in ecclesiastical law for the cause of the accused to be heard without the presence of the accusers. Indeed, if Henry was confident of his innocence, free from any trace of fear about the day set when the rest of the princes had determined to convene in Augsburg, he might then meet [them] with confidence. Once the allegations of each side were aired, he whom neither hatred nor favor could turn aside from law to injustice [i.e., the pope] would bring forth the most just sentence for each side according to ecclesiastical law.

To this they responded that the king would not evade the pope's justice anywhere on earth since he knew him [Gregory] to be a most incorrupt avenger and advocate of innocence and justice. But, they continued, with the anniversary day of the excommunication pressing upon them, the princes of the realm waited in suspense about this disquieting matter, intent upon the outcome. If the king were not absolved before the anniversary day, thereafter he would be held unworthy of royal power according to the law of the realm, and no longer merit an audience to assert his innocence. Only if he were absolved in the meantime from the anathema and received into the grace of ecclesiastical communion would he be bound to seek and prepared to accept everything the pope demanded in the way of satisfaction. Since nothing would be done according to the terms of this agreement, the pope then might demand a full response on whatever day and in whatever place he liked concerning all the crimes his accusers had dredged up and, according to the sentence, whether he would retain his realm, if he cleared himself of the charges, or if convicted, lose it with an even temper.

For a long time the pope resisted, fearing in the young king an inconstant character of mind and proclivity to go wherever flatterers led. But having been overcome by the strength of [their] urging, and the gravity of the decrees, he said, "If he truly repents, let him give over to our keeping the crown and the rest of the royal insignia as proof of a true and heartfelt act of penitence, and declare himself admittedly contumacious and therefore unworthy any longer to bear the name and honor of king." This seemed too harsh to the legates [Henry's representatives]. They strongly insisted that he should temper this demand and not break the shaken reed with the severity of his judgment. At last, with difficulty and displeasure, his assent was obtained to a face to face meeting with the king and if Henry demonstrated true repentance, he might expiate the guilt he had incurred by insulting the Apostolic See, by now obeying its decrees.

Henry came, as he was ordered to, and since that castle had been enclosed by a triple wall, having been received within the space of the second wall, his band of retainers having been left outside, his regalia laid aside, displaying nothing pertaining to the kingship, showing no ceremony, with bare feet and fasting from morning until vespers, he waited for the decision of the Roman Pontiff. He did this a second day, and then a third. On the fourth day, finally having been admitted into the pope's presence, after many opinions were voiced on each side, he was finally absolved from the excommunication under these conditions: that on the day and at the place designated by the pope, he promptly call a general council of the German princes and respond to the accusations they had made, with this pope, if it seemed expedient, presiding as judge. By its [the council's] ruling,[8] it would be decided according to ecclesiastical law whether Henry should retain the realm, if he cleared himself of the charges, or whether, with equanimity, he should be deprived of it, if by proven crimes he be held unworthy of the royal honor. Whether he retained or lost the realm, no vengeance should ever be exacted from any man for this injury. Until the day on which this matter, having been lawfully discussed, would be brought to a conclusion, the king was to use none of the trappings of the royal state, none of the insignia of the royal dignity. He was to do nothing in the way of administering public property according to rightful custom and should make no decrees of any sort. Finally, other than the exaction of royal services by which necessarily he and his [men] were to be supported, he should usurp nothing of the realm, no public property. All those who had sworn loyalty to him should meanwhile be unencumbered and free from the bond of oath and from the duty of keeping faith with him before God and men. He should permanently banish from his company Rutbert bishop of Bamberg, Ulrich of Cosheim, and the rest of those on whose advice he had betrayed himself and public right. But if he, having cleared all obstructions, remained powerful and [even] much strengthened in the realm, nonetheless he would be subject to the Roman pontiff, always obedient to [the pope's] commands and admonishments, consenting to the correction of whatever customs had grown up against ecclesiastical laws in his realm and emerge as a joint-laborer [with the pope] to the best of his ability.

---

[8]Grammatically, Lampert's statement is ambiguous. He could mean that *Gregory* would decide the matter according to ecclesiastical law, but since the matter of the pope's presiding over the council was left open [*si ita expedire videretur,* "if it seemed expedient"], I have translated *eius sententiam* as "its [the council's] ruling."

Finally, if any of these provisions was not fulfilled, this absolution from the excommunication, now so fervently sought, would be void and he would be held a convicted and confessed [sinner], denied an audience for asserting his innocence, and the princes of the entire realm, all freed from their sworn bonds, might proceed to create another king whose election received their consent.

The king accepted the conditions gladly and promised with the most holy affirmations that he would keep them all. Nor did the promiser hold faith lightly. But the abbot of Cluny, since he declined to swear in consequence of his monastic vows, pledged his faith before the eyes of all-seeing God. The bishop of Zeitz, the bishop of Vercelli, Marquis Azzo, and other princes of this gathering also confirmed by their oaths on the relics of the saints that Henry would do what he promised and not be diverted from the decree because of any harshness of things or fickleness of various fortunes afterwards.

The excommunication now lifted, the pope celebrated a solemn mass. The sacred offerings completed, he called the king with the rest of the multitude who were there to the altar and taking in his hands the body of Our Lord, said: "Long ago I received letters from you and your supporters, in which you accused me of occupying the apostolic see through the heresy of simony and of staining my life, both before and after receiving the see, with other like crimes which, according to the canons, would impede my access to Holy Orders. And although I can disprove the charge with the sure attestation of many suitable witnesses—those namely who know the whole course of my life completely from youth and those who promoted me to the see—lest I seem to rely more on human than divine witnesses, in your presence I shall remove any doubt about all these allegations of scandal by making satisfaction. Behold the body of Our Lord which I will consume! Let this be proof today of my innocence so that Almighty God might today cast his judgement either absolving me from every suspicion put forth, if I am innocent or, if I am guilty, may he kill me instantly."[9] Having solemnly spoken these and other awesome words, he entreated God the most just judge to stand as champion of his cause and his innocence. Then he took and ate a piece of the Lord's body. At this

---

[9]Gregory here is performing an "ordeal," calling upon God to judge a matter directly. Gregory's predecessor Alexander II (1061–1073) had already prohibited some forms of the ordeal, and Pope Innocent III at the Fourth Lateran Council would make this prohibition general.

bold sight, the people for a long time hailed him, rejoicing in his innocence and singing praises to God. Finally, when the church fell silent,
turning to the king, the pope said: "Son, if it pleases you, do as you
saw me do. The German princes of the realm battered our ears with
accusations for days, bringing a great mass of capital charges against
you, because of which they judge not only that you should be suspended from the administration of all affairs of state, but also even
from ecclesiastical communion, and from all secular association, until
your last dying breath. They even ask assiduously that I set a day and
place for an audience to be held for canonically judging the charges
they have made against you. And you know very well that human
judgement generally vacillates and that sometimes in public examina-
tions falsities win out over truths, while through the skills of eloquent
men and their resources of speaking and charm, falsity adorned with
the ornament of words is listened to and truth is disparaged without
the support of eloquence. Since, therefore, I very much desire that
you get a fair hearing, because in your distress you sought the help of
the apostolic see as a supplicant, do what I advise. If you know yourself to be innocent and your reputation is assaulted by your rivals
through wrongful denunciation on false charges, fully free the church
from scandal and yourself from the ambiguity of a long controversy:
take this remaining portion of the body of the Lord! [Take it] so that
your innocence proven by the witness of God, every wicked mouth
chattering against you [may] be silenced. With me henceforth the
advocate of your cause and the strong supporter of your innocence,
the princes may be reconciled to you, the kingdom may be restored,
and all those storms of civil war by which your state has so long been
troubled may be calmed forever."

Astonished by this unexpected development, Henry grew agitated,
began to hedge, and having pulled back from the crowd, took faithful
counsel with those closest to him as to what should be done and how
he might avoid the necessity of so awesome a test. At last, recovering
his breath, he began to complain to the pope about the absence of the
princes who as yet had kept complete faith with him in these difficulties. He declared that [the sentence] would be invalid to those supporters of his who had not been consulted, even more so to his absent
accusers, and would have no validity among the incredulous, whatever
amends for proving his innocence he offered to the few who were
there. Therefore, he diligently begged the pope that the whole matter
be put off until a general council and common audience in order that

all those princes, peers of the realm, might judge according to ecclesiastical law as much those debated accusations as the persons and conditions surrounding the accusations, and he might rebut their arguments. Not at all unwillingly, the pope acceded to his request, and having completed the Mass, invited the king to dinner. Having kindly fed Henry and instructed him in all those things he ought diligently to observe, [the pope] dismissed him in peace to those who had remained further outside the castle.

23

POPE GREGORY VII

A Letter to the German Princes

January 1077

This letter sent to the German princes in late January 1077 gives Gregory's rendition of what occurred at Canossa. Since in supporting the papacy many of these princes had taken actions against Henry that would be considered treasonous, Gregory's reconciliation with the king left their lives, lands, and the future of their families in jeopardy. A few years later (in 1080) the pope asserted that he had only restored Henry to communion with the church and had not reinstated him as king. But Henry acted with full royal powers on his return, and, in this letter as well as in subsequent missives, Gregory used the word rex *(king) when referring to him.*

Whereas for love of justice you have made common cause with us and taken the same risks in the warfare of Christian service, we have taken special care to send you this accurate account of the king's penitential humiliation, his absolution and the course of the whole affair from his entrance into Italy to the present time.

According to the arrangement made with the legates sent to us by

The Correspondence of Pope Gregory VII, ed. and trans. Ephraim Emerton (New York: Columbia University Press, 1932; rpt. 1969), 111–13.

you we came to Lombardy about twenty days before the date at which some of your leaders were to meet us at the pass and waited for their arrival to enable us to cross over into that region. But when the time had elapsed and we were told that on account of the troubled times—as indeed we well believed—no escort could be sent to us, having no other way of coming to you we were in no little anxiety as to what was our best course to take.

Meanwhile we received certain information that the king was on his way to us. Before he entered Italy he sent us word that he would make satisfaction to God and St. Peter and offered to amend his way of life and to continue obedient to us, provided only that he should obtain from us absolution and the apostolic blessing. For a long time we delayed our reply and held long consultations, reproaching him bitterly through messengers back and forth for his outrageous conduct, until finally, of his own accord and without any show of hostility or defiance, he came with a few followers to the fortress of Canossa where we were staying. There on three successive days, standing before the castle gate, laying aside all royal insignia, barefooted and in coarse attire, he ceased not with many tears to beseech the apostolic help and comfort until all who were present or who had heard the story were so moved by pity and compassion that they pleaded his cause with prayers and tears. All marveled at our unwonted severity, and some even cried out that we were showing, not the seriousness of apostolic authority, but rather the cruelty of a savage tyrant.

At last, overcome by his persistent show of penitence and the urgency of all present, we released him from the bonds of anathema and received him into the grace of Holy Mother Church, accepting from him the guarantees described below, confirmed by the signatures of the abbot of Cluny, or our daughters, the Countess Matilda and the Countess Adelaide, and other princes, bishops and laymen who seemed to be of service to us.

And now that these matters have been arranged, we desire to come over into your country at the first opportunity, that with God's help we may more fully establish all matters pertaining to the peace of the Church and the good order of the land. For we wish you clearly to understand that, as you may see in the written guarantees described below, the whole negotiation is held in suspense, so that our coming and your unanimous consent are in the highest degree necessary. Strive, therefore, all of you, as you love justice, to hold in good faith the obligations into which you have entered. Remember that we have not bound ourselves to the king in any way except by frank statement—

as our custom is—that he may expect our aid for his safety and his honor, whether through justice or through mercy, and without peril to his soul or to our own.

The Oath of Henry, king of the Germans.

I, Henry, king, within the term which our lord Pope Gregory shall fix, will either give satisfaction according to his decision, in regard to the discontent and discord for which the archbishops, bishops, dukes, counts and other princes of the kingdom of Germany are accusing me, or I will make an agreement according to his advice—unless some positive hindrance shall prevent him or myself—and when this is done I will be prepared to carry it out.

Item: If the same lord Pope Gregory shall desire to go beyond the mountains or elsewhere he shall be safe, so far as I and all whom I can constrain are concerned, from all injury to life or limb and from capture—both he himself and all who are in his company or who are sent out by him or who may come to him from any place whatsoever—in coming, remaining, or returning. Nor shall he with my consent suffer any hindrance contrary to his honor; and if anyone shall offer such hindrance, I will come to his assistance with all my power.

Civil War

24

SIGEBERT OF GEMBLOUX

An Antiking Is Elected
1077

Henry's trip to Canossa forestalled the planned assembly at Augsburg in February, but in March his opponents met in Forchheim and elected the south German prince Rudolf of Swabia king. Gregory later (1080) wrote that he had not approved of Rudolf's election, but several royalist sources

Sigebert of Gembloux, *Chronicon a. 1077,* ed. L. C. Bethmann, in *Monumenta Germaniae historica, Scriptores* 6 (Hannover: Hahn, 1894), 363–64.

depict the princes as acting at the instigation of the pope. Rudolf was crowned in Mainz on March 26, 1077, but the election of a new king did not lead to the outpouring of support Henry's opponents expected. The antiking was forced to withdraw to Saxony, and a civil war began. This account comes from Sigebert of Gembloux's Chronicon. *A monk and teacher at the abbey of Gembloux (near Liège) for most of his life, Sigebert wrote several polemical pieces defending royal and imperial investiture.*

1077. . . . With the Saxon princes who had surrendered to the emperor having been released (through the connivance of those to whom they had been entrusted), the Saxons rose in rebellion at the incitement of Pope Hildebrand. The pope himself, meeting the emperor in Lombardy, absolved him under a false peace. All those who earlier had denied Hildebrand on oath, heaping perjury on top of perjury, now foreswore the emperor and set up Rudolf Duke of Burgundy as king over them. The crown sent to him by the pope had this inscription: "As the rock gave Peter the crown, so Peter gives it to Rudolf."[10] Sigifrid, Archbishop of Mainz, anointed him king and when this was done, the people of Mainz rebelled against them and Rudolf was forced to flee during the night with the archbishop. Pope Hildebrand absolved all those opposing the emperor from their disloyalty and perjury. The emperor, finding the Alpine passes held against him, eluded their ambushes and at once went to Regensburg by way of Aquileia. There he attacked Rudolf, forced him to flee, and renewing his expedition he ravaged Swabia.

---

[10]The inscription is playing off the similarity in Latin between *Petrus,* "Peter," and *petra,* "rock," and Jesus' statement in the Gospel of Matthew (16:18), "You are Peter and upon this rock (*petra*) I will build my church."

25

ROMAN SYNOD

The Decrees against Lay Investiture

November 19, 1078, and March 7, 1080

Gregory was undoubtedly disappointed in Henry's actions after Canossa. The king saw his pressing mission as the restoration of his royal authority, and he accomplished this doggedly over the late spring and early summer. He held court with splendor, rallied moderate princes to his side, assembled a sizable army, and moved against the forces of the antiking. He also invested new bishops, in two cases (Augsburg and Aquileia) overturning the elections of local candidates in order to appoint men of proven loyalty from the royal chapel. The intractability of both Henry and the imperial church—the great majority of bishops in the realm having continued to support the king—frustrated Gregory. This is the essential context for understanding the decrees passed prohibiting lay investiture at the autumn synod of 1078 and the Lenten synod of 1080. The pope's concern was to reform the church in the German lands, and it seemed increasingly clear to Gregory that this could not be accomplished while Henry exercised control over episcopal appointments. Gregory also renewed his excommunication of Henry at the 1080 synod.

Decree of November 19, 1078: Inasmuch as we have learned that, contrary to the establishments of the holy fathers, the investiture with churches is, in many places, performed by lay persons; and that from this cause many disturbances arise in the church by which the Christian religion is trodden under foot: we decree that no one of the clergy shall receive the investiture with a bishopric or abbey or church from the hand of an emperor or king or of any lay person, male or female. But if he shall presume to do so he shall clearly know that such investiture is bereft of apostolic authority, and that he himself shall lie under excommunication until fitting satisfaction shall have been rendered.

Select Historical Documents of the Middle Ages, trans. E. F. Henderson (London: George Bell & Sons, 1892), 365–66.

Decree of March 7, 1080: Following the statutes of the holy fathers, as, in the former councils which by the mercy of God we have held, we decreed concerning the ordering of ecclesiastical dignities, so also now we decree and confirm: that, if any one henceforth shall receive a bishopric or abbey from the hand of any lay person, he shall by no means be considered as among the number of the bishops or abbots; nor shall any hearing be granted him as bishop or abbot. Moreover we further deny to him the favour of St. Peter and the entry of the church, until, coming to his senses, he shall desert the place that he has taken by the crime of ambition as well as by that of disobedience—which is the sin of idolatry. In like manner also we decree concerning the inferior ecclesiastical dignities.

Likewise if any emperor, king, duke, margrave, count, or any one at all of the secular powers or persons, shall presume to perform the investiture with bishoprics or with any ecclesiastical dignity,—he shall know that he is bound by the bonds of the same condemnation. And, moreover, unless he comes to his senses and relinquishes to the church her own prerogative, he shall feel, in this present life, the divine displeasure as well with regard to his body as to his other belongings: in order that, at the coming of the Lord, his soul may be saved.

26

POPE GREGORY VII

A Letter to Hermann of Metz
March 15, 1081

Henry had responded to Gregory's renewal of his excommunication and deposition by holding a council at Brixen on June 25, 1080. Twenty-nine bishops attended, most from northern Italy. The assembly condemned Gregory, calling upon him to abdicate, and elected Wibert of Ravenna as Pope Clement III. In October, Henry defeated the antiking Rudolf, who died of his injuries after the battle on the Elster. As the opposition sought

The Correspondence of Pope Gregory VII, ed. and trans. Ephraim Emerton (New York: Columbia University Press, 1932; rpt. 1969), 166–75.

*to elect another antiking, Gregory wrote this letter defending his second
excommunication of Henry. The recipient, Hermann of Metz, had supported Henry through the early phases of the struggle, and after the king
had returned from Canossa, had pleaded with him to accept papal guid-
ance. When his pleas only aroused Henry's anger, Hermann retreated to
his diocese. But the king interpreted this as rebellion and sent an army to
expel the bishop. Hermann then joined the opposition.*

You ask us to fortify you against the madness of those who babble
with accursed tongues about the authority of the Holy Apostolic See
not being able to excommunicate King Henry as one who despises the
law of Christ, a destroyer of churches and of the empire, a promoter
and partner of heresies, nor to release anyone from his oath of fidelity
to him; but it has not seemed necessary to reply to this request, seeing that so many and such convincing proofs are to be found in Holy
Scripture. . . .

To cite but a few out of the multitude of proofs: Who does not
remember the words of our Lord and Savior Jesus Christ: "Thou art
Peter and on this rock I will build my Church, and the gates of hell
shall not prevail against it. And I will give thee the keys of the kingdom of heaven and whatsoever thou shalt bind on earth shall be
bound in heaven and whatsoever thou shalt loose on earth shall
be loosed in heaven." Are kings excepted here? Or are they not of
the sheep which the Son of God committed to St. Peter? Who, I ask,
thinks himself excluded from this universal grant of the power of binding and loosing to St. Peter unless, perchance, that unhappy man who,
being unwilling to bear the yoke of the Lord, subjects himself to the
burden of the Devil and refuses to be numbered in the flock of Christ?
His wretched liberty shall profit him nothing; for if he shakes off from
his proud neck the power divinely granted to Peter, so much the heav-
ier shall it be for him in the day of judgment.

This institution of the divine will, this foundation of the rule of the
Church, this privilege granted and sealed especially by a heavenly
decree to St. Peter, chief of the Apostles, has been accepted and maintained with great reverence by the holy fathers, and they have given to
the Holy Roman Church, as well in general councils as in their other
acts and writings, the name of "universal mother." They have not only
accepted her expositions of doctrine and her instructions in [our] holy
religion, but they have also recognized her judicial decisions. They

have agreed as with one spirit and one voice that all major cases, all especially important affairs and the judgments of all churches ought to be referred to her as to their head and mother, that from her there shall be no appeal, that her judgments may not and cannot be reviewed or reversed by anyone.

Thus Pope Gelasius, writing to the emperor Anastasius, gave him these instructions as to the right theory of the principate of the Holy and Apostolic See, based upon divine authority:

> Although it is fitting that all the faithful should submit themselves to all priests who perform their sacred functions properly, how much the more should they accept the judgment of that prelate who has been appointed by the supreme divine ruler to be superior to all priests and whom the loyalty of the whole later Church has recognized as such. Your Wisdom sees plainly that no human capacity [*concilium*] whatsoever can equal that of him whom the word of Christ raised above all others and whom the reverend church has always confessed and still devotedly holds as its Head. . . .

Do you remember what the most blessed Apostle Paul says: "Know ye not that we shall judge angels? How much more things that pertain to this life?"

So Pope Gregory[11] declared that kings who dared to disobey the orders of the Apostolic See should forfeit their office. He wrote to a certain senator and abbot in these words:

> If any king, priest, judge or secular personal shall disregard this decree of ours and act contrary to it, he shall be deprived of his power and his office and shall learn that he stands condemned at the bar of God for the wrong that he has done. And unless he shall restore what he has wrongfully taken and shall have done fitting penance for his unlawful acts he shall be excluded from the sacred body and blood of our Lord and Savior Jesus Christ and at the last judgment shall receive condign punishment.

Now then, if the blessed Gregory, most gentle of doctors, decreed that kings who should disobey his orders about a hospital for strangers should be not only deposed but excommunicated and condemned in the last judgment, how can anyone blame us for deposing and excommunicating Henry, who not only disregards apostolic judgments, but so far as in him lies tramples upon his mother the Church, basely

---

[11] Pope Gregory the Great (590–604).

plunders the whole kingdom and destroys its churches—unless indeed it were one who is a man of his own kind? . . .

But now, to return to our point: Is not a sovereignty invented by men of this world who were ignorant of God subject to that which the providence of Almighty God established for his own glory and graciously bestowed upon the world? The Son of God we believe to be God and man, sitting at the right hand of the Father as High Priest, head of all priests and ever making intercession for us. He despised the kingdom of this world wherein the sons of this world puff themselves up and offered himself as a sacrifice upon the cross.

Who does not know that kings and princes derive their origin from men ignorant of God who raised themselves above their fellows by pride, plunder, treachery, murder—in short, by every kind of crime—at the instigation of the Devil, the prince of this world, men blind with greed and intolerable in their audacity? If then, they strive to bend the priests of God to their will, to whom may they more properly be compared than to him who is chief over all the sons of pride? For he, tempting our High Priest, head of all priests, son of the Most High, offering him all the kingdoms of this world, said: "All these will I give thee if thou wilt fall down and worship me."

Does anyone doubt that the priests of Christ are to be considered as fathers and masters of kings and princes and of all believers? Would it not be regarded as pitiable madness if a son should try to rule his father or a pupil his master and to bind with unjust obligations the one through whom he expects to be bound or loosed, not only on earth but also in heaven? Evidently recognizing this the emperor Constantine the Great, lord over all kings and princes throughout almost the entire earth, as St. Gregory relates in his letter to the emperor Mauritius, at the holy synod of Nicaea took his place below all the bishops and did not venture to pass any judgment upon them but, even addressing them as gods, felt that they ought not to be subject to his judgment but that he ought to be bound by their decisions.

Pope Gelasius, urging upon the emperor Anastasius not to feel himself wronged by the truth that was called to his attention said: "There are two powers, O august Emperor, by which the world is governed, the sacred authority of the priesthood and the power of kings. Of these the priestly is by so much the greater as they will have to answer for kings themselves in the day of divine judgment;" and a little further: "Know that you are subject to their judgment, not that they are to be subjected to your will."

In reliance upon such declarations and such authorities, many prelates have excommunicated kings or emperors. If you ask for illustrations: Pope Innocent excommunicated the emperor Arcadius because he consented to the expulsion of St. John Chrysostom from his office. Another Roman pontiff deposed a king of the Franks, not so much on account of his evil deeds as because he was not equal to so great an office, and set in his place Pippin, father of the emperor Charles the Great, releasing all the Franks from the oath of fealty which they had sworn to him. And this is often done by Holy Church when it absolves fighting men from their oaths to bishops who have been deposed by apostolic authority. So St. Ambrose, a holy man but not bishop of the whole Church, excommunicated the emperor Theodosius the Great for a fault which did not seem to other prelates so very grave and excluded him from the Church. He also shows in his writings that the priestly office is as much superior to royal power as gold is more precious than lead. He says: "The honor and dignity of bishops admit of no comparison. If you liken them to the splendor of kings and the diadem of princes, these are as lead compared to the glitter of gold. You see the necks of kings and princes bowed to the knees of priests, and by the kissing of hands they believe that they share the benefit of their prayers." And again: "Know that we have said all this in order to show that there is nothing in this world more excellent than a priest or more lofty than a bishop."

Your Fraternity should remember also that greater power is granted to an exorcist when he is made a spiritual emperor for the casting out of devils, than can be conferred upon any layman for the purpose of earthly dominion. All kings and princes of this earth who live not piously and in their deeds show not a becoming fear of God are ruled by demons and are sunk in miserable slavery. Such men desire to rule, not guided by the love of God, as priests are, for the glory of God and the profit of human souls, but to display their intolerable pride and to satisfy the lusts of their mind. Of these St. Augustine says in the first book of his Christian doctrine: "He who tries to rule over men—who are by nature equal to him—acts with intolerable pride." Now if exorcists have power over demons, as we have said, how much more over those who are subject to demons and are limbs of demons! And if exorcists are superior to these, how much more are priests superior to them!

Furthermore, every Christian king when he approaches his end asks the aid of a priest as a miserable suppliant that he may escape the prison of hell, may pass from darkness into light and may appear at the judgment seat of God freed from the bonds of sin. But who, layman or priest, in his last moments has ever asked the help of an earthly king for the safety of his soul? And what king or emperor has power through his office to snatch any Christian from the might of the Devil by the sacred rite of baptism, to confirm him among the sons of God and to fortify him by the holy chrism? Or—and this is the greatest thing in the Christian religion—who among them is able by his own word to create the body and blood of the Lord? Or to whom among them is given the power to bind and loose in Heaven and upon earth? From this it is apparent how greatly superior in power is the priestly dignity.

Or who of them is able to ordain any clergyman in the Holy Church—much less to depose him for any fault? For bishops, while they may ordain other bishops, may in no wise depose them except by authority of the Apostolic See. How, then, can even the most slightly informed person doubt that priests are higher than kings? But if kings are to be judged by priests for their sins, by whom can they more properly be judged than by the Roman pontiff? . . .

So much for kings and emperors who, swollen with the pride of this world, rule not for God but for themselves. But since it is our duty to exhort everyone according to his station, it is our care with God's help to furnish emperors, kings and other princes with the weapons of humility that thus they be strong to keep down the floods and waves of pride. We know that earthly glory and the cares of this world are wont especially to cause rulers to be exalted, to forget humility and, seeking their own glory, strive to excel their fellows. It seems therefore especially useful for emperors and kings, while their hearts are lifted up in the strife for glory, to learn how to humble themselves and to know fear rather than joy. Let them therefore consider carefully how dangerous, even awesome is the office of emperor or king, how very few find salvation therein, and how those who are saved through God's mercy have become far less famous in the Church by divine judgment than many humble persons. From the beginning of the world to the present day we do not find in all authentic records [seven] emperors or kings whose lives were as distinguished for virtue and piety as were those of a countless multitude of men who despised the world—although we believe that many of them were saved by the mercy of God. Not to speak of Apostles and Martyrs, who among emperors or kings was famed for his miracles as were St. Martin, St. Antony and St. Benedict? What emperor or king ever raised the dead, cleansed lepers or opened the eyes of the blind? True, Holy Church praises and honors the emperor Constantine, of pious memory, Theodosius and Honorius, Charles and Louis, as lovers of justice, champions of the Christian faith and protectors of churches, but she does not claim that they were illustrious for the splendor of their wonderful works. Or to how many names of kings or emperors has Holy Church ordered churches or altars to be dedicated or masses to be celebrated?

Let kings and princes fear lest the higher they are raised above their fellows in this life, the deeper they may be plunged in everlasting fire. Wherefore it is written: "The mighty shall suffer mighty torments." They shall render unto God an account for all men subject to their rule. But if it is no small labor for the pious individual to guard his own soul, what a task is laid upon princes in the care of so many thousand souls! And if Holy Church imposes a heavy penalty upon him who takes a single human life, what shall be done to those who send many thousands to death for the glory of this world? These, although they say with their lips *mea culpa,* for the slaughter of many, yet in their hearts they rejoice at the increase of their glory and neither repent of what they have done nor regret that they have sent their brothers into the world below. So that, since they do not repent with all their hearts and will not restore what they have gained by human bloodshed, their penitence before God remains without the fruits of a true repentance.

Wherefore they ought greatly to fear, and they should frequently be reminded that, as we have said, since the beginning of the world and throughout the kingdoms of the earth very few kings of saintly life can be found out of an innumerable multitude, whereas in one single chair of successive bishops—the Roman—from the time of the blessed Apostle Peter nearly a hundred are counted among the holiest of men. How can this be, except because the kings and princes of the earth, seduced by empty glory, prefer their own interests to the things of the Spirit, whereas pious pontiffs, despising vainglory, set the things of God above the things of the flesh. The former readily punish offenses against themselves but are not troubled by offenses against God; the latter quickly forgive those who sin against them but do not easily pardon offenders against God. The former, far too much given to worldly affairs, think little of spiritual things; the latter, dwelling eagerly upon heavenly subjects, despise the things of this world. . . .

Wherefore let those whom Holy Church, of its own will and with deliberate judgment, not for fleeting glory but for the welfare of multitudes, has called to royal or imperial rule—let them be obedient and ever mindful of the blessed Gregory's declaration in that same pastoral treatise: "When a man disdains to be the equal of his fellow men, he becomes like an apostate angel. Thus Saul, after his period of humility, swollen with pride, ran into excess of power. . . ." Let them ever place the honor of God above their own; let them embrace justice and maintain it by preserving to everyone his right; let them not enter into the counsels of the ungodly, but cling to those of religion with all their hearts. Let them not seek to make Holy Church their maidservant or their subject, but recognizing priests, the eyes of God, as their masters and fathers, strive to do them honor.

If we are commanded to honor our fathers and mothers in the flesh, how much more our spiritual parents! If he that curseth his father or his mother shall be put to death, what does he deserve who curses his spiritual father or mother? Let no princes, led astray by carnal affection, set their own sons over that flock for whom Christ shed his blood if a better and more suitable man can be found. By thus loving their own son more than God they bring the greatest evils upon the Church. For it is evident that he who fails to provide to the best of his ability so great and necessary an advantage for our holy mother, the Church, does not love God and his neighbor as befits a Christian man. If this one virtue of charity be wanting, then whatever of good the man may do will lack all saving grace.

But if they do these things in humility, keeping their love for God and their neighbor as they ought, they may count upon the mercy of him who said: "learn of me, for I am meek and lowly of heart." If they humbly imitate him, they shall pass from their servile and transient reign into the kingdom of eternal liberty.

27

LANFRANC, ARCHBISHOP OF CANTERBURY

A Letter to Hugh Candidus

ca. 1084–1085

Henry took an army to Italy in 1081 and began building up the power of his supporters. Using diplomacy, gifts, and siege warfare, he slowly brought a significant portion of the Roman nobility and clergy over to his side. On June 3, 1083, the king took the basilica of Saint Peter's, Gregory having retreated to the Castel Sant'Angelo, a fortress on the banks of the Tiber. By early 1084 twelve cardinals had defected to Henry. Wibert was consecrated by these cardinals and enthroned as Pope Clement III on March 24. Gregory called in his Norman ally Robert Guiscard, duke of Apulia and Calabria, but the army he brought to Rome so violently sacked the city that the population forced Gregory to retreat to Salerno. This letter of Lanfranc, Archbishop of Canterbury, registers the impact of Henry's victory in Rome on public opinion and reveals the predicament of Christians throughout Europe. Lanfranc was responding to a letter of Hugh Candidus supporting Clement III and seeking to collect on his behalf a lucrative English tithe traditionally paid to the papacy called "Peter's Pence."

Lanfranc to Hu[gh].

I have received and read the letter which you sent me by the messenger who brought you mine: certain passages which I found in it displeased me. I disapprove of your attacks on Pope Gregory, calling him Hildebrand and labeling his legates "thick-heads," and your readiness to laud Clement with such a paean of praise. It is written that a man should not be praised in his lifetime, nor his neighbour slandered. What men are like now in the sight of God and what they shall be like hereafter is still unknown to them. But it is my conviction that the glorious emperor did not undertake such a mighty achievement without

---

The Letters of Lanfranc, Archbishop of Canterbury, edited with a facing page English translation from the Latin text by Helen Clover and Margaret Gibson (Oxford Medieval Texts, 1979), 165–67. Reprinted by permission of Oxford University Press.

good cause, nor could he have gained so notable a victory without great assistance from God. I am not in favour of your coming to England unless you first get permission to come from the king of the English. Our island has not yet repudiated the one nor decided whether to obey the other. When the case for both sides has been heard (if that should happen), it will be possible to see more clearly what is to be done.

28

POPE GREGORY VII

Deathbed Testament

ca. 1085

Gregory did not live long after his retreat from Rome; he died in Salerno on May 25, 1085. This is his deathbed testament, probably recorded over his last few days by one of his chaplains. The text survives in a collection of letters at Hildesheim that contains items relating to Bishop Anselm of Lucca, an active member of the papal reform circle, and Countess Mathilda of Tuscany. H. E. J. Cowdrey has suggested that the testament may well have been composed within or directed to this important circle of Gregory's supporters shortly after the pontiff's demise.

When he was at Salerno, our lord Pope Gregory of blessed and worthy memory was gripped by the grave illness from which he later died. The Roman bishops and cardinals who were there, assembled around him, were asking and begging him to reveal whom he wished proposed as his successor in the pontifical office. After pondering this a short while, he himself said these words to them: "Elect as pope anyone of these three—namely, the bishop of Lucca [Anselm], the bishop of Ostia [Odo], or the archbishop of Lyons [Hugh]—that you will have been able to consider."

Die Hannoversche Briefsammlung: 1. Die Hildesheimer Briefe, ed. C. Erdmann and N. Fickermann, in *Monumenta Germaniae historica, Briefe der Deutschen Kaiserzeit* 5 (Weimar: H. Böhlaus, 1950), no. 35, 75–76.

Having been asked about those who had been excommunicated, he responded: "Excepting Henry, called king, and the archbishop of Ravenna [Wibert] — unless, of course, as may seem better to you, they shall have come to you [to make] worthy and canonical amends — and [excepting] all the chief persons who aided their iniquity and impiety with their advice and help, I absolve and bless all the rest who believe without doubt that I hold this spiritual power in the name of the apostle Saint Peter."

In addition to this, reminding them of many things, he gave them this order: "On behalf of almighty God and by the authority of the blessed apostles Peter and Paul, I command you to accept no one as pontiff unless he shall have been canonically elected and ordained by the authority of the holy fathers."

When he was at his end, his last words were: "I loved justice and I hated iniquity, therefore I die in exile."

Compromise

29

IVO, BISHOP OF CHARTRES

A Letter to the Apostolic Legate Hugh of Lyon
1097

Ivo of Chartres (ca. 1040–1115) began his ecclesiastical life as a regular canon in Beauvais and was elected bishop of Chartres by its clergy and people in 1090. A gifted theologian and scholar of canon law, Ivo passionately promoted reform efforts but did not hesitate to criticize what he saw as the excesses of the papal party. He wrote this letter in 1097 in response to a papal legate's command not to consecrate as bishop of Sens the man, Daimbert, who had been elected. The previous bishop of Sens, Richerius (1062–1096), had refused to accept Pope Urban II's subordination of the see to the primacy of the archbishop of Lyon, and clearly the

---

Yves de Chartres, *Correspondance*, ed. Jean Leclercq (Paris: Société d'Edition "Les Belles Lettres," 1949), no. 60, 1: 238–54.

status of the see of Sens was the issue lurking just below the surface of this dispute.

To Hugh, Archbishop of Lyon, legate of the Apostolic See, Ivo humble minister of the church of Chartres [sends] greetings and submission.

It was done as you commanded: and thus we have refrained from consecrating the bishop-elect of Sens and, in obedience to apostolic authority, we have circulated your letters to the other bishops of the province. Accordingly we advise and ask your discretion that in other respects you more sparingly bind us with the chain of apostolic obedience, lest by placing insupportable burdens on our shoulders you make any lapse of obedience either an impossibility or a necessity of ruling. For it may be easy for you to fight by threatening from afar, but it is even easier for us here present to kill a dangerous adversary with the sword. Thus we wish to observe the interdicts and mandates promulgated by the apostolic see for the defense of the faith, for the improvement of the faithful, for the correction of the wicked, for the prohibition of menacing and future evils, and as we were prepared to, God willing, weather whatever adversity necessary for their defense. But you so resolutely demand compliance with those [mandates] which are neither good nor bad—when safety is least endangered by their non-observance and least aided by their observance—and you minimize or modify as you will those [mandates] which antiquity sanctified, custom observed, and the sacred authority of the venerable fathers [of the church] confirmed. Because your prudence ought to attend to those [mandates] that serve the well-being of those whom you ought to serve in all you do, ought one observe more closely the teaching of those [fathers] or show stronger obedience to these [others]: to those holy fathers who have spoken to us through their writings? Or to you, whose purpose seems anything but following these teachings or honoring their vestiges?

I don't say that new ordinances should not be promulgated against new abuses, but I say what Pope Zosimus said to the inhabitants of Narbonne: "The authority of this see is not able to concede or change something against the statutes of the fathers; for among us with undisturbed roots lives antiquity, to which the decrees of the fathers ordain reverence." In the book called Diurnus of that same pontiff, [we find] this profession of the Roman pontiff: "I promise not to invent, diminish, change, or add any novelty to the tradition which was served and passed on to me by my most wise predecessors, but with my whole mind and in every effort to observe and venerate fervently as their disciple and successor, all that I learned of what was handed down canonically." [Ivo goes on to cite six other authorities making the same point.]

When, therefore, these as well as other general traditions so unanimously hold for consecration by the metropolitan, we wondered why you were striving to replace old traditions and customs with private laws and new traditions, ordering the bishop-elect of Sens to be presented to you before his consecration so that he might promise obedience and submission to your primatial right—something which up to now neither antiquity nor custom has required in the province of Sens or in other provinces. Thus Pope Nicholas, among other things, wrote to Rudolph bishop of Bourges about usurping any further right of primacy for himself: "Primates or patriarchs have no privileges beyond those held by the rest of the bishops except what the sacred canons concede or what early tradition conferred on these, so that the privileges of the churches are preserved according to the canons of the second council of Nicaea." But if by the privilege of your legateship you direct him to be presented to you, when he was not accused by anyone before us or you, [you act] not as pope Leo did with his vicar, Anastasius Bishop of Thessalonica. [For he demanded] only that priests bring the name of the elect to the notice of his provincials, so as not to undermine proper elections with difficulties and delays. From what we have heard, [the bishop-elect of Sens] is a person of noble birth, well educated, well regarded by acquaintances, who has discharged the office of deacon in his church, and was freely elected without any dissent. But if in any way he concedes to these exactions [that you demand], it may be said that he bought his consecration by some gift of words or service.

You write that the aforesaid bishop-elect accepted the investiture of his see from the king, but we neither know nor have heard this from anyone who saw it. Nevertheless, even if he did, we do not know how the inclusion or omission [of the investiture] might interfere with the faith or holy religion since it does not have the force of a sacrament in constituting a bishop and we do not see in the least that kings are prohibited by apostolic authority from conferring the see after a canonical election. For we read that supreme pontiffs of holy memory have sometimes intervened with kings on behalf of those having been elected to churches in order that their sees be conceded by those kings, while other pontiffs have delayed consecrations because the royal concession had not yet followed the election. . . . When kings intend not to bestow anything spiritual, but only either to assent to the wishes of those petitioning or to confer on those elected the ecclesiastical estates and other worldly goods which derive from the liberality of the king—what should it matter if the concession is made by hand, by command, by word, or by staff? Thus Augustine [writes] in his sixth treatise on the Gospel of John, in the first part: "By what right do you defend the estates of the Church? By a divine or human right? Divine law is from scripture, human ones from the laws of the realm. When each possesses what he possesses, is it not by human right? For in divine right: the land is the Lord's and its fullness is his. Concerning human right it is said: this is my estate, this is my house, this slave is mine. Abolish the laws of the emperors and who will dare say: this estate is mine, this slave is mine, this house is mine? . . ."

But if these things [rules against investiture] were established by eternal law, it would not be in the power of rulers to judge strictly according to them in some instances and in others to relax them mercifully so that some remain in offices bestowed in a manner contrary to what they prescribe. For truly, since it is the prohibition of rulers that in fact makes these acts illicit, so too the remission of them by rulers according to their own judgment is licit. We see no one, or almost no one, condemned for this sort of transgression, but [we do see] many disquieted, many churches despoiled, many scandals arisen, and division between the priestly and royal powers, and without concord between these, human affairs can be neither safe nor secure. We also see wretched bishops and abbots neither willing nor able to free themselves from their wrecked traditions or from defensive reparations, but only intent upon this: that they are able to make themselves the friends of any pompous big-mouth by whose commerce they may be able to defend themselves in one way or another. Also, many prelates elected freely and canonically, because they are impeded in taking office by delays and difficulties, having from their own resources paid for mediators and procurators, lest they suffer some shameful rejection, sometimes end up blemishing their consecration with the sin of simony. When, therefore, every ecclesiastical institution must retreat to the law in order to pursue the good of souls, the excesses of these institutions ought either to be corrected severely, so that they are effective in procuring this spiritual welfare or, in other cases, quietly exposed, lest proper spiritual and temporal matters be impeded by such legalities. I do not say this because I wish to question the authority of the apostolic see, or reject its sound decisions, or cast doubt on the rulings of my superiors, if they are based upon the living knowledge and clearer authority of the ancient fathers. But I do wish, along with many other pious persons, that the ministers of the Roman church, like prudent doctors, would devote themselves to curing the truly grave illnesses so that we don't have to hear from their scoffing critics, "Straining after a gnat you end up swallowing a camel; you pay tithes on mint, bitter herbs, cumin, and fennel, while neglecting the weightier matters of the law" (Matt. 23:23–24). Throughout nearly the whole world we see offences and crimes openly perpetrated, but—look!—are they stopped by you with your great scythe of justice? Because examples of such offences are either well known to you or ignored by you, it is not my place to devote a special sermon to them. You will have already seen which of these crimes or similar cases merits action.

Indeed, now my pen turns especially to this one: that you permit the bishop-elect of the church of Sens, if nothing against the sacred canons be discovered in him, to be consecrated according to ancient custom. [I ask this] because we neither wish nor ought to cede even a small right pertaining to our church, holding with Cyprian who said, "How dangerous it is to cede any right or power in divine matters, sacred scripture declares: after Esau had lost his birthright, he was not able to regain what he once ceded." But if you shall heed our petition, we will zealously persuade that one having been consecrated to recognize the primacy of the church of Lyon, and thus defer to your primacy, and to show all due reverence according to the tradition of the fathers. If he shall not have acquiesced to our persuasions, we nevertheless do not withdraw from those things that the Roman see shall have demanded. If, however, you will not accede to our petition and, against our wishes, some schism shall have arisen, I can say with confidence [that it is] neither "my iniquity, nor my sin" [Ps. 58.5], something you will not be able to say to yourself. . . .

30

EMPEROR HENRY V AND POPE CALIXTUS II

The Agreements of Worms

1122

The controversy over investiture outlived both Gregory and Henry. Several more confrontations between popes and monarchs, however, helped clarify the central concerns of both sides and suggested grounds for compromise. Particularly important was the English king Henry I's grudging abandonment of investiture in 1107 in return for acknowledgment of his right to receive homage from bishops and abbots for the temporalities of their sees or abbeys. The pope at that time, Pascal II (1099–1118), also came to a compromise with the Capetian monarchs of France and had reason to be optimistic that some agreement would be reached with the empire. He had supported the rebellion of Henry IV's son Henry against the emperor in 1104–1105, and the death of the elderly ruler in 1106 seemed to clear the way for a rapprochement. But Henry V turned out to be as attached as his father to what he perceived as royal prerogatives: Several failed negotiations, and an attempt to extort an agreement through kidnapping the pope, wore out both sides. The agreement between Emperor Henry V and Pope Calixtus II, reached outside of Worms on September 23, 1122, left many issues unaddressed, but it did establish some peace.

In the name of the holy and indivisible Trinity, I, Henry, by the grace of God august emperor of the Romans, for the love of God and of the holy Roman church and of the lord Pope Calixtus, and for the good of my soul, remit to God and to the holy apostles of God, Peter and Paul, and to the holy catholic church, all investiture by ring and staff. And I grant that there may be canonical election and free consecration in all churches that are in my kingdom and empire. All the possessions and regalia of Saint Peter which were seized from the beginning of this discord until this day, whether in the time of my father or also in mine,

---

Monumenta Germaniae historica, Legum sectio IV: Constitutiones et acta publica imperatorum et regum, vol. 1 (Hannover: Hahn, 1893), 159–61.

and which I now hold, I restore to the holy Roman church. As to those which I do not hold, moreover, I will faithfully assist in their restoration. With the counsel of princes and according to justice, I will also return to the holy Roman church the possessions of all other churches and princes, and of all other lay and clerical persons, which were lost in that war and which I hold. Those that I do not hold, I will faithfully aid in restoring. And I grant true peace to our lord Pope Calixtus and to the holy Roman church and to all those who are or have been on its side. In matters where the holy Roman church shall demand aid, I will grant it; and in matters about which it makes complaint to me, I will render justice. All these things were done with the consent and counsel of the princes whose names are written below: Adalbert archbishop of Mainz; F[rederick] archbishop of Cologne; H. bishop of Ratisbon; O. bishop of Bamberg; B. bishop of Speyer; H. of Augsburg; G. of Utrecht; Ou. of Constance; E. abbot of Fulda; Henry, duke; Frederick, duke; S. duke; Pertolf, duke; Margrave Teipold; Margrave Engelbert; Godfrey, count Palatine; Otto, count Palatine; Berengar, count. I, Frederick, archbishop of Cologne and arch-chancellor authenticated this.

I, bishop Calixtus, servant of the servants of God, grant to you beloved son, Henry—by the grace of God august emperor of the Romans—that the elections of the bishops and abbots of the German kingdom, that pertain to the kingdom, shall take place in your presence, without simony and without any violence; so that if any discord shall arise between the parties concerned, you, with the counsel and judgment of the metropolitan [archbishop] and the co-provincial [bishops], may give consent and aid to the more worthy party. The one elected, moreover, without any exaction may receive the regalia from you through the scepter [i.e., through the instrumentality of royal power], and may render those things owed to you by law for these things. One having been consecrated in other parts of the empire [i.e., Burgundy and Italy] may receive the regalia from you through the scepter within six months and may render those things owed to you by law for these things. All those things recognized to pertain to the Roman church are excepted [from the preceding]. Concerning matters about which you make complaint to me or ask for aid, I assuredly will help you according to the duty of my office. I give true peace to you and to all who are or have been on your side during this discord.

3

The Consequences of Reform

The consequences of the reform movements and the investiture conflict were numerous and far-reaching for both laity and clergy. They
were worked out over the twelfth century and into the early thirteenth.
Laypeople who had actively worked for and supported reform sought a
greater engagement with their faith. The laity's desire for a more
intense spiritual life flowered into new movements and institutional
forms, some of which gained acceptance, whereas others were condemned as heretical. Two activities were increasingly central to lay
spiritual experience. The first was preaching. Listening to sermons
became an important part of lay religiosity, and the desire to preach
marked many lay movements. The second was armed pilgrimage, or
crusade. The effects of reform on the clergy were equally far-reaching.
To be sure, many of the original problems that had sparked the reform
movement seemed intractable, such as the purity of the clergy, and
many of the original solutions, such as canonical election, proved im-
practical. But new norms for clerical behavior were established, and
attempts were made at greater supervision, even if complaints about
the lives and characters of priests continued. Bishops were expected to
exert more control over the ecclesiastical institutions and personnel of
their dioceses. A new image of the ideal bishop emerged that combined religious virtue with administrative efficiency and emphasized
the defense of the rights and privileges of the church, even unto death.
The biggest change in the postreform church, however, was in the
power of the papacy. Gregory VII had articulated an expansive theory
of papal authority, but it was his successors who built the institutions of
governance capable of realizing these claims. The new power of papal
monarchy helped foster spiritual initiatives, but its bureaucratic under-
pinnings also generated criticism and cynicism. Finally, while the
papacy had become a monarchy, monarchs refused to relinquish claim
to the holy. Temporal rulers made greater claims to wield and embody
holiness, and this too was a legacy of the investiture conflict.

Lay Engagement with the Faith

31

BAUDRI OF DOL

The Preaching of Robert of Arbrissel

ca. 1118

Reformers emphasized preaching as an important duty of the clergy, and the popular response to Ariald's words in the Pataria movement demonstrated the power sermons could have. The career of Robert of Arbrissel reveals how the preaching of reform developed into a broader mission to the laity. Born in Brittany around 1045, Robert was the son and grandson of priests, an embodiment of what the reformers most criticized in clerical life. He became, however, an ardent preacher of reform. After a long period of study in Paris, he was invited by Bishop Sylvester of Rennes to help reform the clergy of his diocese, and Robert spent four years as archpriest of Rennes campaigning against clerical marriage and simony there. Those resisting change gained the upper hand when Bishop Sylvester died in 1093, and Robert withdrew, first to study in Angers and then to become a hermit in the forest of Craon. This selection from the life of Robert, written by Baudri of Dol, reveals how laypeople sought out his words even in remote places. So many people were moved by his admonitions to abandon their former lives and follow Christ that Robert ended up founding first a house of regular canons at La Roë and then a rather unique monastery at Fontevraud, where men and women lived together under the rule of an abbess. He continued to preach and gather followers into new institutions until his death in 1116. One of his earliest converts, a noblewoman named Petronilla of Chemillé, whom Robert had appointed as abbess of Fontevraud, asked Baudri archbishop of Dol to write this account of Robert's life just after his death (ca. 1118). A contemporary of Robert, Baudri knew him from their schooling

Baudri of Dol, *The Life of Robert of Arbrissel,* chap. 2–3, in *Robert of Arbrissel (ca. 1045–1116): A Medieval Religious Life,* ed. and trans. Bruce L. Venarde (Washington, D.C.: Catholic University of America Press, 2003), 12–14.

at Angers. Before becoming archbishop of Dol, Baudri was abbot of the Benedictine monastery of Bourgueil, very near Fontevraud.

The day came when Robert, renouncing the world, sped away to the wilderness he had so long desired, in the company of a certain priest. He stayed in the forest, rejecting the society of men to become the companion of beasts. Who could worthily recount how completely and with what savagery he raged against himself, how many and severe the tortures he inflicted on himself, with what grim horrors he weakened himself? For beyond the outwardly visible—like wearing a pig-hairshirt, shaving his beard without water, scarcely knowing but one blanket, refraining altogether from wine and from rich or fine food, abusing natural frailty by rarely getting half a night's sleep—there was also internal conflict, a kind of roar in his mind and a sobbing in the depths of his soul, which you could think cruel and impious and susceptible to no lasting remedy, and which, many murmured, was too much, impossible for claylike brittleness [of human flesh: Job 4:19–20]. He quarreled with God in incomparable wailing and pledged his whole self as a sacrifice. Mild and gentle with everyone, Robert was an implacable enemy at war with himself alone.

To crowds of comers—for a great many people came to see him— he was cheerful and pleasant, friendly and courteous, prudent in doubtful matters, quick in replies. He gave off something like the perfume of divine expressiveness, for few were his equal in eloquence. So it happened that many, after hearing him, were heartstruck and renounced their wicked ways. Some returned home, improved by his preaching; others desired to linger with him and asked to enter into his service and stay with him as permanent companions. He would have fled these throngs of his own accord and hidden himself away all alone had he not been afraid to incur blame on that account. For he had read *Let him who hears say, "Come"* (Rev. 22:17). Therefore it was incumbent on him to mete out the talent granted him, which the Lord coming from the wedding demanded with interest.[1] He realized that he should gather many together, and give them something to eat, lest they grow weak along the way, since certain of them had come a long distance (Mark 8:1–3). Those gathered together were called "regulars," who tried to live in the way of the early Church under a rule.

---

[1] Baudri's metaphor combines elements from Luke 12:36 and Matt. 25:14–30.

And therefore this multitude [lit. swarm], fleeing from the enticements of the world, became a congregation of canons. Robert presided over them, teaching them in the honeyed way of a very wise bee. They built a common dwelling and lovingly embraced his authority in teaching.

It happened in those days that the Roman pontiff Urban II had come to Gaul as urgent affairs required and turned to stop in Angers. He heard about Robert, for such great light ought not be hidden under a bushel (Matt. 5:15, Mark 4:21, Luke 11:33). The pope ordered him to be summoned, for he eagerly desired a conversation with Robert. Urban prepared to solemnly consecrate a church, to which ceremony you might think the whole of the earth flocked. The pope ordered Robert to speak to this great gathering and he commanded him to use his accustomed discourse.

Robert spoke brilliantly to the people, and his words pleased the Lord Pope immensely, for Urban understood that the Holy Spirit had opened up his mouth (Ps. 51:15). Next the pontiff ordered and enjoined on Robert the office of preaching; he insisted on the duty of obedience when Robert hesitated a little. The pope appointed Robert his second as God's word-scatterer and urged him to pursue this mission wherever he went.

Henceforth, Robert began to apply himself diligently to his commission from the highest pontiff, traversing the territories of neighboring dioceses. He was honored by all, both because he was worthy of honor and because God's grace manifestly went along with him. His language was neither arid nor idle and a retinue praiseworthy in words and deeds entrusted itself to it. Robert practiced what he preached, lest he himself be condemned straightaway as worthless for having preached to others what he did not fulfill himself. Such a great crowd attached itself to him that the number of his canons might almost have been thought nothing at all. The number would exceed reckoning if only a tenth of the worshipers had joined the community of canons. . . .

32

WALTER MAP

Description of the Waldensians

ca. 1180–1183

Robert of Arbrissel had his critics and was never canonized because of scandalous rumors about his relations with women, but he and his followers managed to remain in the good graces of the church. Not all popular preachers, however, fared so well. In 1173 a wealthy merchant of Lyons named Waldes (or Valdès) gave away all his belongings and started caring for the poor. He quickly attracted followers, and some of them came to Rome in 1179 to seek papal approval for their religious initiative. This account is from Walter Map, a cleric from the court of the English king Henry II and his royal delegate to the Third Lateran Council. Walter had studied in Paris, and his account of the Waldensians, as well as his prose style, registers a rather fulsome pride in his own learning. Yet, the passage also reveals how the voluntary poverty and humility of the Waldensians unsettled and threatened clerics like Walter. Pope Alexander III, however, reacted more positively to the Waldensians, praising the vows of poverty they had taken but forbidding them to preach without the permission of a priest. For disregarding the latter, they were condemned as heretics and excommunicated by Pope Lucius III in 1184.

I saw in the Council at Rome under the celebrated Alexander, third pope of that name, Waldenses, illiterate laymen, called after their founder Waldes, a citizen of Lyons on the Rhone. These presented to His Holiness a book written in the French tongue, containing the text and a gloss of the Psalter and of very many books of both the Old and New Testaments. They besought him with great importunity to confirm the licence of their preaching, because they seemed to themselves experts, although they were mere dabblers. For it usually

---

Walter Map, *De nugis curialium (Courtiers' Trifles)*, dist. 1, chap. 31, trans. Frederick Tupper and Marbury Bladen Ogle (London: Chatto & Windus, 1924), 76–79, with emendations.

happens that birds which do not see the subtle snares or nets believe that there is free passage everywhere. Do not those persons who are occupied all their days with sophistries—men who can ensnare and yet can scarce be snared, and who are ever delvers in the deep abyss—do not those men, in fear of disfavor, profess with reverence to bring forth all things from God, whose dignity is so lofty that no praises or no merits of prayers can attain to that height, unless sovereign mercy has borne them aloft? On every dot of the divine page [of scripture], noble thoughts are wafted on so many wings, and such wealth of wisdom is amassed that he alone to whom God has given something [to draw with] may drink from the full [well]. Shall, therefore, in any wise pearls be cast before swine, and the word given to laymen who, as we know, receive it foolishly, to say nothing of their giving what they have received? No more of this, and let it be rooted out! . . . I, the least of the many thousand who were called to the council, derided them, wondering that there should be any debate or doubt about their petition, and when I was summoned by a certain great bishop, to whom the mightiest of popes had entrusted the charge of their confessions, I sat down, "a mark for their arrows" (Lam. 3:12). After many masters of the law and men of learning had been gathered, there were brought before me two Waldenses who seemed the chief of their sect, eager to argue with me about the faith, not for the love of seeking the truth, but so that by convicting me of error, they might stop my mouth as of "one speaking lies." I sat full of fear—I confess—lest, under the pressure of my sins, the power of speech in so great a council should be denied me. The bishop ordered me, who was ready to reply, to try my eloquence against them. At the outset, I suggested the easiest questions, which anybody should be able to answer, for I knew that when an ass is eating thistles, its lips disdain lettuce: "Do you believe in God the Father?" They answered, "We believe." "And in the Son?" They replied, "We believe." "And in the Holy Spirit?" Their reply still was "We believe." I kept on, "In the Mother of Christ?" And they again, "We believe." Amid the derisive shouts of all, they withdrew in embarrassment, which was richly deserved, because they were ruled by none and sought to be made rulers, like Phaethon who "did not know the names of his horses" (Ovid, Metamorphoses 2.192).

These have nowhere a fixed abode, but wander about in pairs, barefooted, clad in sheepskins, possessing nothing, "having all things in common" like the apostles, naked following the naked Christ. Their beginnings now are humble because they can find no entrance anywhere, but, should we let them in, we should be driven out. Let him who does not believe hear what has already been said of like sort. In these times of ours which we condemn and deride, there are doubtless those who wish to keep faith, and should they be put to the test, they would, as in times gone by, lay down their shepherd, Lord Jesus. But because we have been led astray or lured away by a strange sort of zeal, our times have grown as base as though of iron.

33

POPE INNOCENT III

A Rule for the Third Order of the Humiliati

June 7, 1201

One of the other groups condemned as heretics along with the Waldensians in Lucius III's 1184 decree was the Humiliati (or "humble ones"). The movement emerged in northern Italy, and it included both clerics and laypeople, men and women, married and single people. The earliest sources on the Humiliati's vision of the apostolic life are vague, but it seems to have involved cultivating simple ways, wearing plain clothing, and meeting for prayer. Despite the 1184 condemnation, the Humiliati continued to grow, and at the very end of the century they approached the papacy to ask for a reconsideration of their way of life. After considerable scrutiny, Pope Innocent III recognized the Humiliati and approved their three branches, or orders. Clerics living in communities constituted the First Order, men and women living under a rule of religious life were the Second Order, and married or single laymen and laywomen remaining in their homes and there pursuing a religious life formed the Third Order. This Third Order was a truly novel form of religious life, and it was much copied in the thirteenth century, most notably by the Mendicants (the Franciscan and Dominican orders). In this letter of June 7, 1201, Pope Innocent III laid out how those professed in the Third Order of the Humiliati were to live.

G. G. Meersseman, *Dossier de l'ordre de la pénitence au XIIIe siècle* (Fribourg: Éditions universitaires, 1961), 276–82.

Innocent to his beloved sons Guy of Porta Orientale, C. of Monza, A. of Como, N. of Pavia, G. of Brescia, I. of Bergamo, I. of Piacenza, I. of Lodi, R. of Cremona and other ministers of the same order and their brothers and sisters.

By the duty of our pastoral office, it is incumbent upon us to sow holy religion, to foster it once planted, and, as much as we can, confirm all people, together and individually, in pious resolution lest, deprived of Apostolic support, they do not thrive but instead falter and either return [like dogs] to vomit or lose ardor in seeking the good. Thus, when your plan for religious life [*propositum*] had been presented to us, we diligently had it read in our and our brothers' presence, and with certain amendments having been made, we approved it—although for greater precaution, we had this letter inserted, word for word.

1. You propose to maintain humility of heart and gentleness of manners in serving God. Thus the Lord in the Gospel said: "Learn from me, for I am gentle and humble-hearted and your souls will find relief" (Matt. 11:29). [You propose] to serve all prelates of the church in obedience. Thus, the Apostle: "Obey your leaders and submit to them; they are watching over you, as men who must render an account for your souls" (Heb. 13:17). For there is no true humility when an overseer forsakes obedience. Patience in adversity is very much needed (Heb. 10:34) for enduring with equanimity the evils done to you by others. Thus in the Gospel the Lord [said], "The old law said an eye for an eye, a tooth for a tooth. But I say to you, do not resist the man who wrongs you, but if someone slaps you on the right cheek, give him the left as well," and "If a man forces you to go one mile, go with him another two," and "if someone sues you for your shirt, let him have your coat as well" (Matt. 5:39–41)....

2. Moreover, "above all things, brothers, do not swear, either 'by heaven' or 'by earth' or by anything else. When you say yes or no, let it be plain yes or no without exposing yourselves to judgment," as the Apostle James said (James 5:12). You should not swear an oath unwisely or on a whim, but only when an important undertaking compels you out of urgent necessity. Christ in the Gospel as well as James in his letter prohibited indiscriminate and spontaneous swearing, saying, "Our forefathers were told, do not break your oath and keep your oath to God. I, however, say to you, do not swear by anything—not by heaven, for it is God's throne, nor by earth, for it is his footstool, nor by Jerusalem, for it is the city of the great King, nor by your own head, because you cannot turn one hair of it white or black"

(Matt. 5:33–36). . . . The apostle teaches, however, that one may licitly take an oath when necessary, saying: "Men swear by someone or something greater than themselves and the oath settles all dispute" (Heb. 6:16). . . .

3. Finally, as the Lord said: "In all things, do unto others as you would have them do to you. Strive to enter by the narrow gate, because the way is wide and the gate narrow that leads to life and few are those who enter it. The way to perdition, on the contrary, is wide and spacious and many enter upon it" (Matt. 7:12–15). "Therefore, do penance," (Matt. 3:3) and "do not sin" (1 Cor. 15:35). "Then you will have peace with all men" (Rom. 12:18).

4. Give back interest and any other ill-gotten gains, for a sin is not remitted unless what was given is restored. And make satisfaction for other injuries. As the Lord says in the Gospel: "If, when you are bringing your gift to the altar, you suddenly remember that your brother has a grievance against you, leave your gift where it is before the altar. First go and make your peace with your brother, and only then come back and offer your gift" (Matt. 5:24).

5. Do not possess tithes, since laymen are not allowed to hold these. Thus, Gregory VII: "By apostolic authority we prohibit laymen from possessing tithes, which canonical authority demonstrates to have been given for pious uses. Even if they accepted them from a bishop or religious or any other person, unless they returned them to the church, let them know that they have committed a crime, a sacrilege and risk eternal damnation." Therefore, you should turn over tithes and first-fruits to clerics, to whom they belong, for canonical distribution according to the disposition of the diocesan bishop. For it is proper to give tithes as the Lord instructs in the Gospel: "Alas for you, lawyers and Pharisees, hypocrites! You pay tithes of mint and dill and cumin, but you have overlooked the weightier demands of the Law, justice, mercy, and good faith. It is these you should have practiced without neglecting the others" (Matt. 23:23). From those fruits and earnings which you keep, give alms and everything beyond your just needs, give to the poor, just as the apostle says, "not relieving others at a cost of hardship to yourselves" (2 Cor. 8:13). Thus also the Lord in the Gospel said: "Nevertheless, what remains give in alms, and all is clean" (Luke 11:41). Similarly, "Do not store up treasure on earth, where it grows rusty and moth-eaten, and thieves break in to steal it. Store up treasure in heaven, where there is no moth and no rust to spoil it, no thieves to break in and steal" (Matt. 6:19–20).

6. "Do not set your hearts on the world or anything in it. Anyone

who loves the world is a stranger to the Father's love. Everything the world affords, all that panders to the appetites or entices the eyes, all the glamour of its life, springs not from the Father but from the world. And that world is passing away with all its allurements. But he who does God's will stands for evermore"—thus the apostle John bears witness (1 John 2:15–17). The apostle James also speaks of these things, saying: "Do you not know, adulterers, that the love of this world is enmity to God? Whoever chooses to be the world's friend makes himself God's enemy" (James 4:4). To those of you, however, who are joined in matrimony, the Lord enjoins you not leave your wives except for unchastity (Matt. 19:9). But the apostle says, "a man owes a debt to his wife, and similarly the wife to her man, unless perhaps by consent they abstain" (1 Cor. 7:3–5).

7. Unless prevented by infirmity, weakness, or work, let everyone fast on the fourth and sixth days of the week, except on Pentecost, from Christmas to Epiphany, and on other solemnities.

8. On non-fasting days, be content with a midday meal and dinner; be sparing with food and temperate in drink. For the Lord says in the Gospel: "Be vigilant, lest your hearts be weighed down in dissipation and drunkenness and the cares of this life" (Luke 21:34).

9. When you come to table, before you eat, say the Lord's Prayer; and after eating, say it again.

10. You should observe seven canonical hours—namely: Matins, Prime, Terce, Sext, None, Vespers, and Compline—since, according to the prophet, you praise the Lord seven times a day (Ps. 118:164). At each hour, say the Lord's Prayer seven times because of the seven gifts of the Holy Spirit. Say the Creed—that is, "I believe in God"—at Prime and Compline.

11. Clothing should be neither too fine nor too shabby, but such that it is not deemed irreligious, because neither pretended squalor nor exquisite elegance becomes a Christian.

12. As is already manifest in your customs, if anyone in your community lacks worldly goods or is hindered by illness, assist him with temporal things as well as all necessary care.

13. When one of your members dies, announce it to the brothers and let everyone come to the funeral. Let each one say the Lord's Prayer and "God Have Mercy on Me" twelve times for his soul, so that with the help of God you strive and determine to persevere in and preserve your order and way of life.

14. So that your way of life is sustained by the prayers of your brothers, each of you should every day say the Our Father three times for

the living and three times for the deceased of your community, and once for the peace of the church and the whole Christian people.

15. It will be your custom to gather together every Sunday to hear the word of God in a suitable place. There, one or another of the brothers, of proven faith and experienced in religion, those who "are powerful in word and deed" (Luke 24:19), with the permission of the diocesan bishop, should offer words of exhortation to those gathered to hear the word of God, admonishing and encouraging them in honorable ways and pious works. They are not, however, to speak about the articles of faith or the sacraments of the church.

16. We prohibit any bishop, in contravention of what is set out above, to impede the brothers in any way from offering words of exhortation, for as the apostle says, "do not stifle the spirit" (1 Thess. 5:19).

17. Therefore, you my beloved sons in the Lord should follow the form of life that we have diligently examined, prudently corrected, and salutarily approved, "with a pure heart, a good conscience, and genuine faith" (1 Tim. 1:5), so that you may deserve to receive eternal mercy from him who is the rewarder of all merit and the examiner of hearts.

34

ROBERT THE MONK

The Calling of the First Crusade

ca. 1100–1125

Another highly significant development in lay piety that emerged from the reform movement was the idea of armed pilgrimage or crusade. The reformers' concerns with purity and their vision of papal authority, popular enthusiasm for an apostolic or Christ-centered life, and continuing ecclesiastical interest in controlling violence came together in a unique way at the council of Clermont in 1095. After promulgating reform decrees against simony and lay control of churches and tithes, Pope

Dana C. Munro, *Urban and the Crusaders* (Philadelphia: Department of History of the University of Pennsylvania, 1895), 5–7.

*Urban II gave a sermon that sparked what became the First Crusade.
Five accounts of this sermon survive, and historians have long studied
and debated their evidence for what exactly the pope envisioned. These
excerpts are from Robert the Monk's version of the speech. Writing in the
first quarter of the twelfth century, Robert was a monk at Reims who
based parts of his account on a work called* The Deeds of the Franks, *written by a crusader in the army of the Norman leader Bohemund.*

Oh, race of the Franks, race from across the mountains, race chosen
and beloved by God—as shines forth in very many of your works—
set apart from all nations by the situation of your country, as well as
by your catholic faith and the honor of the holy church! To you our
discourse is addressed and for you our exhortation is intended. We
wish you to know what a grievous cause has led us to your country,
what peril threatening you and all the faithful has brought us.

From the confines of Jerusalem and the city of Constantinople[2] a
horrible tale has gone forth and very frequently has been brought to
our ears, namely, that a race from the kingdom of the Persians, an
accursed race, a race utterly alienated from God, a generation forsooth
which has not directed its ear and has not entrusted its spirit to God,
has invaded the lands of those Christians and has depopulated them
by the sword, pillage and fire; it has led away a part of the captives
into its own country, and a part it has destroyed by cruel tortures; it
has either entirely destroyed the churches of God or has appropriated
them for the rites of its own religion. They destroy the altars, after
having defiled them with their uncleanness. They circumcise the
Christians, and the blood of the circumcision they either spread upon
the altars or pour into the bases of the baptismal font. When they wish
to torture people by a base death, they perforate their navels, and
dragging forth the extremity of the intestines, bind it to a stake; then
with flogging they lead the victim around until the viscera having
gushed forth the victim falls prostrate upon the ground. Others they
bind to a post and pierce with arrows. Others they compel to extend
their necks and then, attacking them with naked swords, attempt to
cut through the neck with a single blow. What shall I say of the abom-
inable rape of the women? To speak of it is worse than to be silent.

---

[2]*Constantinople:* Seat of the Byzantine emperor, who had appealed to the West for
military help against the Seljuk Turks after the Byzantine defeat at the battle of Manzik-
ert in 1071.

The kingdom of the Greeks is now dismembered by them and deprived of territory so vast in extent that it can not be traversed in a march of two months. On whom therefore is the labor of avenging these wrongs and of recovering this territory incumbent, if not upon you? You, upon whom above other nations God has conferred remarkable glory in arms, great courage, bodily activity, and strength to humble the hairy scalp of those who resist you.

Let the deeds of your ancestors move you and incite your minds to manly achievements; the glory and greatness of king Charles the Great [i.e., Charlemagne], and of his son Louis, and of your other kings, who have destroyed the kingdoms of the pagans, and have extended in these lands the territory of the holy church. Let the holy sepulchre of the Lord our Saviour, which is possessed by unclean nations, especially incite you, and the holy places which are now treated with ignominy and irreverently polluted with their filthiness. Oh, most valiant soldiers and descendants of invincible ancestors, be not degenerate, but recall the valor of your progenitors.

But if you are hindered by love of children, parents and wives, remember what the Lord says in the Gospel, "he that loveth father or mother more than me, is not worthy of me" (Matt. 10:37). "Every one that hath forsaken houses, or brethren, or sisters, or father, or mother, or wife, or children, or lands for my name's sake shall receive an hundred-fold and shall inherit everlasting life" (Matt. 19:29). Let none of your possessions detain you, no solicitude for your family affairs, since this land which you inhabit, shut in on all sides by the seas and surrounded by the mountain peaks, is too narrow for your large population; nor does it abound in wealth; and it furnishes scarcely food enough for its cultivators. Hence it is that you murder one another, that you wage war, and that frequently you perish by mutual wounds. Let therefore hatred depart from among you, let your quarrels end, let wars cease, and let all dissensions and controversies slumber. Enter upon the road to the Holy Sepulchre;[3] wrest that land from the wicked race, and subject it to yourselves. That land which as the Scripture says "floweth with milk and honey," was given by God into the possession of the children of Israel.

Jerusalem is the navel of the world; the land is fruitful above others, like another paradise of delights. This the Redeemer of the human race has made illustrious by His advent, has beautified by resi-

---

[3] *Holy Sepulchre:* The tomb in Jerusalem where Jesus was laid after his crucifixion.

dence, has consecrated by suffering, has redeemed by death, has glorified by burial. This royal city, therefore, situated at the centre of the
world, is now held captive by His enemies, and is in subjection to
those who do not know God, to the worship of the heathens. She
seeks therefore and desires to be liberated, and does not cease to
implore you to come to her aid. From you especially she asks succor,
because as we have already said, God has conferred upon you above
all nations great glory in arms. Accordingly undertake this journey for
the remission of your sins, with the assurance of the imperishable
glory of the kingdom of heaven.

When Pope Urban had said these and very many similar things in
his urbane discourse, he so influenced to one purpose the desires of
all who were present, that they cried out, "It is the will of God! It is the
will of God!"

35

BERNARD OF CLAIRVAUX

On the New Knighthood

ca. 1128–1136

*The response to Urban's sermon was phenomenal. Thousands of ordi-
nary people set out for Jerusalem, in addition to five armies led by
French and Norman knights. Most of the unarmed and poor commoners
were massacred in Asia Minor, but the organized militias conquered
Jerusalem in 1099. They set up secular principalities, which may not
have been what Pope Urban had in mind, but the call to crusade and
crusading indulgences continued to be powerful tools in papal politics.
For lay religiosity, however, the primary importance of crusading was
the Christianization of knighthood. By providing a sanctioned and valor-
ous outlet for knightly violence, the crusades allowed ecclesiastical leaders to influence and transform the values of European nobles. While most*

Bernard of Clairvaux: In Praise of the New Knighthood, trans. Conrad Greenia in *The
Works of Bernard of Clairvaux,* vol. 7: *Treatises III* (Kalamazoo, Mich.: Cistercian Publications, 2000), 45–48.

elites simply cultivated more "chivalrous" behavior, some created new knightly religious orders. The most successful of these, the Knights Templars, was founded in 1118 by Hugh of Payen, a knight from Champagne fighting to defend the Kingdom of Jerusalem established by the crusaders in the Holy Land. The Templars and other military orders blended elements of discipline and devotional life from traditional Benedictine monasticism with the mission of bearing arms in defense of Christianity. This description of their ideals and way of life comes from one of their earliest supporters, the great Cistercian abbot Bernard of Clairvaux. He wrote his tract In Praise of the New Knighthood *for the Templars' founder Hugh of Payen between 1128 and 1136.*

And now as a model, or at least for the shame of those knights of ours who are fighting for the devil rather than for God, we will briefly set forth the life and virtues of these cavaliers of Christ. Let us see how they conduct themselves at home as well as in battle, how they appear in public, and in what way the knight of God differs from the knight of the world.

In the first place, discipline is in no way lacking and obedience is never despised. As Scripture testifies, the undisciplined son shall perish and rebellion is as the sin of witchcraft, to refuse obedience is like the crime of idolatry (1 Sam. 15:23). Therefore they come and go at the bidding of their superior. They wear what he gives them, and do not presume to wear or to eat anything from another source. Thus they shun every excess in clothing and food and content themselves with what is necessary. They live as brothers in joyful and sober company, without wives or children. So that their evangelical perfection will lack nothing, they dwell united in one family with no personal property whatever, careful to keep the unity of the Spirit in the bond of peace. You may say that the whole multitude has but one heart and one soul to the point that nobody follows his own will, but rather seeks to follow the commander.

They never sit in idleness or wander about aimlessly, but on the rare occasions when they are not on duty, they are always careful to earn their bread by repairing their worn armor and torn clothing, or simply by setting things to order. For the rest, they are guided by the common needs and by the orders of their master.

There is no distinction of persons among them, and deference is shown to merit rather than to noble blood. They rival one another in mutual consideration, and they carry one another's burdens, thus fulfilling the law of Christ. No inappropriate word, idle deed, unrestrained laugh, not even the slightest whisper or murmur is left uncorrected once it has been detected. They foreswear dice and chess, and abhor the chase; they take no delight in the ridiculous cruelty of falconry, as is the custom. As for jesters, magicians, bards, troubadours and jousters, they despise and reject them as so many vanities and unsound deceptions. Their hair is worn short, in conformity with the Apostle's saying, that it is shameful for a man to cultivate flowing locks. Indeed, they seldom wash and never set their hair—content to appear tousled and dusty, bearing the marks of the sun and of their armor.

When the battle is at hand, they arm themselves interiorly with faith and exteriorly with steel rather than decorate themselves with gold, since their business is to strike fear in the enemy rather than to incite his cupidity. They seek out horses which are strong and swift, rather than those which are brilliant and well-plumed, they set their minds on fighting to win rather than on parading for show. They think not of glory and seek to be formidable rather than flamboyant. At the same time, they are not quarrelsome, rash, or unduly hasty, but soberly, prudently and providently drawn up into orderly ranks, as we read of the fathers. Indeed, the true Israelite is a man of peace, even when he goes forth to battle.

Once he finds himself in the thick of battle, this knight sets aside his previous gentleness, as if to say, "Do I not hate those who hate you, O Lord; am I not disgusted with your enemies?" (Ps. 138:21). These men at once fall violently upon the foe, regarding them as so many sheep. No matter how outnumbered they are, they never regard these as fierce barbarians or as awe-inspiring hordes. Nor do they presume on their own strength, but trust in the Lord of armies to grant them the victory. They are mindful of the words of Maccabees,[4] "It is simple enough for a multitude to be vanquished by a handful. It makes no difference to the God of heaven whether he grants deliverance by the hands of few or many; for victory in war is not dependent on a big army, and bravery is the gift of heaven" (1 Macc. 3:1–20). On numerous occasions they had seen one man pursue a thousand, and two put ten thousand to flight.

Thus in a wondrous and unique manner they appear gentler than lambs, yet fiercer than lions. I do not know if it would be more appropriate to refer to them as monks or as soldiers, unless perhaps it

---

[4]*Maccabees:* The Maccabees were a family famed in Old Testament history as heroic fighters, first against the Hellenistic king Antiochus Epiphanes (who occupied Jerusalem and plundered its temple in 167 B.C.E.) and later against the Romans.

would be better to recognize them as being both. Indeed they lack neither monastic meekness nor military might. What can we say of this, except that this had been done by the Lord, and it is marvelous in our eyes. These are the picked troops of God, whom he has recruited from the ends of the earth; the valiant men of Israel chosen to guard well and faithfully that tomb which is the bed of the true Solomon,[5] each man sword in hand, and superbly trained to war.

[5]*the true Solomon:* i.e., Jesus Christ. Solomon was king of Israel ca. 965–926 B.C.E. Famed for his rebuilding of the temple in Jerusalem and for his wisdom, Solomon late in his reign fell into apostasy.

The Clergy

36

MARTIN AND ANZIVERGA

Gift to Their Son Adam

May 30, 1060

and

JOHN

Lease to Martin dal Danno

February 1156

The reform movement was quite successful in defining and disseminating new standards of conduct for the clergy. These new ideals may not have entirely changed how clerics lived (see Document 37), but they did change how they represented themselves in public documents. Wives and children of priests, who appeared frequently in documents before the reform, vanished from them in the twelfth century.

Codice diplomatico padovano, ed. A. Gloria, 3 vols. (Venice: Deputazione di storia patria per le Venezie, 1877–1881), 1: 212 (no. 181); *Regesto della chiesa cattedrale di Modena,* ed. E. P. Vicini, 2 vols. (Rome: Maglione, 1931–1936), 1: 359 (no. 461).

Before: Martin and Anziverga. In the name of eternal God. In the year from the incarnation of our Lord, Jesus Christ, 1060 on [May 30]. To you, Adam, deacon, beloved son and our friend, we—Martin, priest, and Anziverga his woman, residing in the village called Castelnovo, both of us professing to live by the Roman law—your father and mother, and your benefactors, being present we say to those present that today, because of our love for you, we confirm in your right and power the following: namely, one quarter part of the houses and all things which we are known to have in the county of Vicenza, in the place and territory of that village of Castelnovo, within the village and castle and outside of them, within their bounds and territories. Indeed, we the aforementioned—Martin, priest, and Anziverga—to confirm this charter of donation accept from you—the aforesaid Adam, deacon, beloved son and our friend—a counter-gift.

After: John. 1156, in the month of February. John, priest, having been constituted pastor of the church of S. Andrea and S. Rufino in the place called Porcile, conceded through a charter of precarial lease, to Martin dal Danno, son of Geminiano Capelli, of Mugnano, and to his legitimate male heirs, sons and nephews, down to the third generation . . . one piece of arable land in the place called Casolaro. . . . [For this] he is to pay every year in the month of March 3 denarii of Lucca in Porcile; let the penalty [should he not pay the rent] be 30 solidi in denarii of Lucca. Done in the castle of Porcile. . . .

37

EUDES RIGAUD, ARCHBISHOP OF ROUEN

Visitation to Inspect His Clergy

1248

Enforcing the new code of conduct for the clergy was the job of bishops who were enjoined to visit the churches under their care and correct lapses. Records of such episcopal visitations survive from the thirteenth century, and they reveal continued concern over the entire range of

The Register of Eudes of Rouen, trans. Sydney M. Brown, ed. Jeremiah F. O'Sullivan (New York: Columbia University Press, 1964), 24, 27.

issues raised by reformers about clerical deportment: sexual relations with women, exacting fees for spiritual services (such as the blessing mentioned here called "churching," which was administered to women when they came to church after the birth of a child), wearing lay attire, and engaging in other worldly pursuits. This entry from the register of Eudes Rigaud, archbishop of Rouen in France, records his visitation of 1248. "Item" here means "on the same day."

January 19. We visited the priests of the deanery of Foucarmont, whom we convoked at St.-Léger. We found that the priest of Nesle was defamed of a certain woman who is said to be with child by him; that he is engaged in trade; that he treated his own father, who owns the advowson [patronage right] of his church, in a most disgraceful manner; that he fought a certain knight with drawn sword, making a great clamor, and was supported by a following of friends and relations. Item, the priest at Basinval is ill famed of a certain woman, and although he has been disciplined by the archdeacon he continues to have relations with her and even takes her to the market; he also frequents taverns. Item, the priest at Vieux-Rouen is ill famed of incontinence, and although he was disciplined by the archdeacon in the matter of one woman he has not ceased to carry on with others; he goes about girt with a sword and wears unseemly clothes. Item, the priest at Bouafles does not wear a gown, is ill famed of a certain woman, and sells his grain at a rather advanced price because of the poor harvest. Item, the priest at Hesmy, reported to be a leper, is ill famed of incontinence. Item, the priest at Ecotigny plays at dice and quoits, and was unwilling to publish the marriage banns of a certain person who had not restored his father's legacy; he frequents taverns, is ill famed of incontinence, and continues his evil ways although he has been disciplined. Item, the priest at Mesnil-David is disobedient and has his children at home and a concubine elsewhere; item, two women fell upon each other in his house; they fought with each other and because one was fond of roses the other cut down the rose bushes. Item, the priest at St.-Riquier [-en Rivière] is [ill famed] of a certain married woman, his parishioner. Item, the priest at La Pierre [-sur-Yères] ran away with a certain woman and, although suspended, continued to celebrate Mass. We ordered the above to appear before us at a later day, when we will deal with them. . . .

January 20. We visited the deanery of Neufchâtel, convoking the priests of that deanery to Lucy. We found that the priest at Ormesnil is defamed of the daughter of a certain lady; he has been disciplined by the archdeacon and has sworn to regard his church as resigned. Item, Adam, the priest at Nesle [-Hodeng] was disciplined by the archdeacon for drunkenness and incontinence. Item, the priest at Sommery does not keep residence in his church as he should and goes riding about as a vagabond. Item, the priest at Mesnil-Mauger is reported to buy and sell horses and other commodities. Item, the priest at Ménonval is ill famed of a certain woman. Item, the priest at Fesques attends neither [deanery] chapters nor synods. Item, Master Robert of Houssay, parson at Conteville, is publicly known for drunkenness, incontinence, squandering, and annoying his parishioners, and for non-residence. Item, the priest at Maucomble attends the assizes and courts held by laymen. Item, the priest at Lucy exacts thirteen pence from every churched woman, and if a child die before the churching, he does not wish to receive the mother for churching until she shall have paid thirteen pence. Item, the priest at Haucourt buys and holds farms from the abbess of Bival; the priest at Noyers has no gown; the priest at Louvicamp keeps hunting dogs; the priests at Sausseuzemare and at Beaubec have no gowns. We warned them as we had done in the other deaneries, and we imposed a penalty for failure to wear a gown and enjoined the dean to exact this penalty without mercy. This day, we spent the night at Aliermont.

Bishops

38

A Disputed Election at Auxerre

1116

Canonical or "free" election of bishops began to occur in dioceses throughout Europe in the wake of the investiture conflict, but things didn't always go smoothly. Disputes over who had a right to participate in an election were common, and even when this was uncontested, the electors

---

Gesta pontificum Autissiodorensium, chap. 54, in *Bibliothèque historique de l'Yonne,* 2 vols., ed. L.-M. Duru (Auxerre and Paris: Société des sciences historiques et naturelles de l'Yonne, 1850–1863), 1: 410–11.

often disagreed as to who was the best candidate. Across the twelfth cen-
tury, many cases—such as the one described here—were appealed to
Rome. The great number of appeals led ultimately to the system of papal
provision (the pope simply appointing the bishop) that emerged in the
thirteenth century. This system was justified by the notion that all
churches and all property of churches came under papal authority, but it
was resisted throughout the later Middle Ages.

When it became known that lord Humbald, venerable bishop of Auxerre, had died on his way to Jerusalem, a majority of the clerics of his
church, having waited a seemly amount of time, elected as bishop the
aforesaid abbot [Hugh, of the Cluniac monastery of Saint Germain of
Auxerre]. But the provost of that church, a man by the name of Hulgerius, and some canons [of the cathedral] along with him, nominated
the aforesaid provost [Hulgerius] and resisted the election of that holy
man. They even went so far as to get the help of King Louis, son of
the reigning King Philip, in their opposition, so that he refused to concede all the rights and privileges pertaining to the see to anyone but
Hulgerius. Then Hugh, forced and constrained by his electors, and his
adversaries went to the threshold of the apostles [Rome], in order that
the election be adjudicated by the pope. The most merciful Lord, giver
of all good things, against whom there is no wisdom or counsel, gave
such grace to the reverend abbot in the eyes of the pope (who at that
time was named Paschal) that he merited receiving episcopal consecration from him. Then, having made peace with his adversaries,
Hugh returned home with great joy and was embraced by his clergy
and people. He met the count of that region, who at that time was
being held captive at Mansello and who later took the Carthusian
habit, and found him glad to confirm his election. He visited even the
French king, who had earlier opposed him, and soon after his arrival
was at peace with him. Thereafter, Hugh lived in his diocese with as
much purity of soul as humility. . . .

39

WILLIAM OF NEWBURGH

Account of Thomas Becket's Martyrdom

ca. 1190–1198

Since the Worms agreements had not resolved the fundamental tensions between ecclesiastical and secular authority, conflicts continued to arise—and bishops were often at the center of them. One of the most dramatic was between King Henry II of England (1154–1189) and Thomas Becket, archbishop of Canterbury (1162–1170). Thomas was not from a particularly wealthy family, but through education and administrative service came first into the favor of Archbishop Theobald of Canterbury and then into the favor and service of Henry. Their long personal relationship made their subsequent conflict all the more bitter. This account by William of Newburgh (d. 1198), a canon of the Augustinian priory of Newburgh in Yorkshire, was written in the closing years of the twelfth century. The author's distance from the royal court surely contributed to the impartiality of this account, remarkable for its even-handed censure of both sides. It conveys the escalating series of slights to honor and calculated provocations that drove the dispute to a bloody crescendo in Canterbury cathedral. Becket came to be venerated as a saint throughout Europe, and his career had all the hallmarks of the "ideal" postreform bishop: heroic defense of the rights and privileges of his church, humble submission to papal authority and collaboration in papal reforming efforts, intense personal piety, and martyrdom. William's account of the conflict also offers interesting evidence of how the investiture conflict was viewed a century later, as he suggests that Pope Gregory VII "would have acted with more mildness" than Thomas.

Before the year had expired in which the council[6] was held, the displeasure of the king of England waxed hot against the venerable

---

[6]The Council of Westminster (October 1163), at the behest of King Henry, had approved a series of provisions bringing clerics who committed crimes under the jurisdiction of royal, rather than ecclesiastical, courts.

Church Historians of England, trans. J. Stevenson, 8 vols. (London: [s.n.], 1853–1870), vol. 4, pt. 2, 465–67, 478–80.

Thomas, archbishop of Canterbury, the unhappy source of the numerous and excessive evils which ensued. This Thomas was born in London; he was a man of acute understanding and competent eloquence as well as elegant in person and manner; he was second to none in despatch of business; he had been conspicuous in the service of Theobald, archbishop of Canterbury, and had received from him the archdeaconry of Canterbury on the promotion of Roger to the see of York. But when Henry the second, on the demise of Stephen,[7] (as it has been before observed,) succeeded to his hereditary kingdom, he was unwilling to be without the services of a man fit to stand before kings, so he made Becket his royal chancellor. Being elevated to this office, he executed it with such reputation, and gained at the same time such high regard and distinctions from his prince, that he seemed to share the government with him.

Some years had elapsed in his secular services, when, behold, he was enlisted in ecclesiastical warfare, and obtained, through the royal pleasure, the see of Canterbury. After a time, considering piously and sagaciously the responsibility of so high an honour, he on a sudden exhibited such a change in his habit and manners, that some observed, "This is the finger of God," and others, "This is a change effected by the hand of the Most High." In the second year after his advancement, he was present at the council of Tours,[8] where, as it is reported, being pricked by remorse of conscience, he privately resigned into the pope's hands the primacy, having, as it were, received it not regularly and canonically, but by the agency and hand of the king. The pope, approving of the transaction, restored to him his pastoral office by virtue of his ecclesiastical power, and healed the wounded conscience of the scrupulous prelate.

The bishops having returned from the council to their several sees, the royal and priestly powers began to be at variance in England, and no small commotion arose concerning the prerogatives of the clergy. For it was intimated by the judges to the king, (who was diligently occupied in the concerns of the state, and who had ordered all malefactors to be indiscriminately banished,) that many crimes against public order, such as thefts, rapines, and murders, were repeatedly committed by the clergy, to whom the correction of lay jurisdiction

---

[7] *Stephen:* King Stephen (1135–1154) was the nephew of King Henry I (1100–1135) of England, who died without a legitimate male heir.

[8] A council convened at Tours in France in 1163 by Pope Alexander III, chiefly in order to combat heresy but also to muster support for his papacy in the wake of a schism.

could not be extended. Finally, it was declared, in his presence, that during his reign more than a hundred murders had been committed by the clergy in England alone. Hereupon the king waxing extremely indignant, enacted laws, in the heat of his passion, against ecclesiastical delinquents, wherein he gave evidence of his zeal for public justice, though his severity rather exceeded the bounds of moderation. Still, however, the blame and the origin of the king's excess in this point attaches only the prelates of our times, inasmuch as it proceeded entirely from them. For since the sacred canons enjoin that not only flagitious clerks, that is, such as are guilty of heinous crimes, but even such as are only slightly criminal, shall be degraded—and the church of England contains many thousands such, like the chaff innumerable amid the few grains of corn—what number of the clergy have there been deprived of this office during many years in England? The bishops, however, while anxious rather to maintain the liberties or rights of the clergy than to correct and root out their vices, suppose that they do God service, and the church also, by defending against established law those abandoned clergy, whom they either refuse or neglect to restrain, as their office enjoins, by the vigour of canonical censure. Hence the clergy, who, called into the inheritance of the Lord, ought to shine on earth, in their lives and conversation, like stars placed in the firmament of heaven, yet take licence and liberty to do what they please with impunity; and regard neither God, whose vengeance seems to sleep, nor men who are placed in authority; more especially as episcopal vigilance is relaxed with respect to them, while the prerogative of holy orders exempts them from all secular jurisdiction.

Thus, when the king had enacted certain statutes against the chaff of the holy order, that is to say, for the examination or punishment of the guilty clergy, in which perhaps (as it has been said) he exceeded the bounds of moderation, he conceived that they would be fully ratified could they be confirmed by the consent of the bishops. Therefore, having assembled the prelates, to procure their sanction by any means whatsoever, he so allured the whole of them with the exception of one, by blandishments, or terrified them with alarms, that they deemed it necessary to yield to and obey the royal pleasure, and set their seals to the enactment of these new constitutions—I say, with the exception of one, for the archbishop of Canterbury was alone inflexible, and remained unshaken by every assault. Upon this, the king's fury became more vehemently incensed against him, in proportion as he appeared more indebted to the royal munificence for what had been given and received. Hence the king became hostile to him, and, seeking every occasion to attack him, demanded an account of everything he had formerly done in the kingdom, in his office as chancellor. The archbishop, with intrepid freedom, replied, that having discharged his secular duties, he had been completely transferred to the church by the prince in whose service he had been engaged, and that matters of bygone date ought not to be urged against him, but this more for a pretext than for truth. While the causes of the king's anger became daily more aggravated, on the day when the archbishop was to answer at large to the allegations against him, he ordered the solemn office of St. Stephen—"The princes sat and spake against me, and sinners persecuted me"—to be duly chanted before him at the celebration of mass. Afterwards he entered the court, carrying in his hand the silver cross, which was usually borne before him; and when some of the bishops present wished to undertake the office of carrying the cross before their metropolitan, he refused, and, although entreated, he would not allow any other to bear the cross in that public assembly. The king, being already enraged beyond measure at these circumstances, had an additional incentive to his fury; for in the following night the archbishop secretly escaped, and passed beyond the sea, where, being honourably received by the king, the nobility, and the bishops of France, he took up his residence for a time. The king of England, consequently, was furiously enraged at his absence; and, giving way to unbridled passion more than became a king, took an unbecoming and pitiful kind of revenge, by banishing all the archbishop's relations out of England. . . .

In the year one thousand one hundred and seventy from the delivery of the Virgin, which was the seventeenth of the reign of Henry the second, the king caused his son Henry, yet a youth, to be solemnly anointed and crowned king at London, by the hands of Roger, archbishop of York. For the king not being yet appeased, the venerable Thomas, archbishop of Canterbury, was still an exile in France, though the Roman pontiff and the king of France had interested themselves extremely to bring about a reconciliation. The moment Thomas heard of this transaction, jealous for his church, he quickly informed the pope of it (by whose favour and countenance he was supported), alleging that this had taken place to the prejudice of himself and his see: and he obtained letters of severe rebuke, for the purpose of correcting equally the archbishop of York, who had performed the office in another's province, and the bishops, who, by their presence, had sanctioned it. The king, however, continued but a short time in England after the coronation of his son, and went beyond the sea; and when urged by the frequent admonitions of the pope and the earnest entreaties of the illustrious king of France, that he would, at least, condescend to be reconciled to the dignified exile, after a seven years' banishment, he at length yielded; and a solemn reconciliation took place between them, which was the more desired and the more grateful in proportion to the time of its protraction.

While the king, therefore, continued abroad, the archbishop, by royal grant and permission, returned to his diocese; having in his possession, unknown to the king, letters obtained from the pope against the archbishop of York, and the other prelates who had assisted at that most unfortunate coronation; which was the means of breaking the recently concluded peace, and had become the incentive to greater rage. These letters, for the suspension of the prelates, preceded him into England; and he followed them himself, burning with zeal for justice, but God knows whether altogether according to knowledge; but it is not allowed by my insignificance, by any means, to judge hastily of the actions of so great a man. I think, nevertheless, that the blessed pope Gregory [VII], during the slight and yet fresh reconciliation of the king would have acted with more mildness, and would have deemed it proper, (considering the time and terms of their reunion,) to have winked at things, which might have been endured without injury to the Christian faith, according to the language of the prophet, "The prudent shall keep silence at that time; for it is an evil time" (Amos 5:13). Therefore, what was done by the venerable pontiff at this juncture, I neither think worthy of commendation, nor do I presume to censure; but this I say, that, if this holy man, through rather too great a fervency of zeal, was guilty of some little excess, yet was it all purged out in the fire of that holy suffering which is known to have ensued. . . .

The bishops, on account of the offence before mentioned (which I could wish to have remained unnoticed at the time), being suspended, at the instance of the venerable Thomas, from all episcopal functions, by the authority of the apostolic see, the king was exasperated by the complaints of some of them, and grew angry and indignant beyond measure, and losing the mastery of himself, in the heat of his exuberant passion, from the abundance of his perturbed spirit, poured forth the language of indiscretion. On which, four of the bystanders, men of noble race and renowned in arms, wrought themselves up to the commission of iniquity through zeal for their earthly master; and leaving the royal presence, and crossing the sea, with as much haste as if posting to a solemn banquet, and urged on by the fury they had imbibed, they arrived at Canterbury on the fifth day after Christmas, where they found the venerable archbishop occupied in the celebration of that holy festival with religious joy. Proceeding to him just as he had dined, and was sitting with certain honourable personages, omitting even to salute him, and holding forth the terror of the king's name, they commanded (rather than asked, or admonished him) forthwith to remit the suspension of the prelates who had obeyed the king's pleasure, to whose contempt and disgrace this act redounded. On his replying that the sentence of a higher power was not to be abrogated by an inferior one, and that it was not his concern to pardon persons suspended not by himself, but by the Roman pontiff, they had recourse to violent threats. Undismayed by these words, though uttered by men raging and extremely exasperated, he spoke with singular freedom and confidence. In consequence, becoming more enraged than before, they hastily retired, and bringing their arms, (for they had entered without them,) they prepared themselves, with loud clamour and indignation, for the commission of a most atrocious crime. The venerable prelate was persuaded by his friends to avoid the madness of these furious savages, by retiring into the holy church. When, from his determination to brave every danger, he did not acquiesce, on the forcible and tumultuous approach of his enemies, he was at length dragged by the friendly violence of his associates to the protection of the holy church. The monks were solemnly chanting vespers to Almighty God, as he entered the sacred temple of Christ, shortly to become an evening sacrifice. The servants of Satan pursued having neither respect as Christians to his holy order, nor to the sacred place, or season; but attacking the dignified prelate as he stood in prayer before the holy altar, even during the festival of Christmas, these truly nefarious Christians most inhumanly murdered him. Having done the deed, and retiring as if triumphant, they departed with unhallowed joy. Recollecting, however, that perhaps the transaction might displease the person in whose behalf they had been so zealous, they returned to the northern parts of England, waiting until they could fully discover the disposition of their monarch towards them.

The frequent miracles which ensued manifested how precious, in the sight of God, was the death of the blessed prelate, and how great the atrocity of the crime committed against him, in the circumstances of time, place, and person. Indeed, the report of such a dreadful outrage, quickly pervading every district of the western world, sullied the illustrious king of England, and so obscured his fair fame among Christian potentates, that, as it could scarcely be credited to have been perpetrated without his consent and mandate, he was assailed by the execrations of almost all, and deemed fit to be the object of general detestation. . . .

The Papacy

40

POPE ADRIAN IV

A Papal Bull

1156

Letters were key tools in the papal reform effort. Gregory VII's carried the commands of the Holy See far and wide throughout Europe. The breadth of Gregory's correspondence is even more impressive given the rudimentary administrative apparatus of the Roman court, or curia, *in his time. His immediate successors, however, built the institutions of governance that realized many of the claims to papal sovereignty that Gregory had asserted in theory. They developed efficient systems of justice and finance. Critical to all these institutions was the papal chancery, which developed into a highly sophisticated bureaucratic tool under Pope Pascal II (1099–1118) and his chancellor, John of Gaeta (later Pope Gelasius II). The chancery codified set formulas for papal letters and privileges, which allowed the pope and his staff to handle the growing volume of appeals and business with greater efficiency. Safeguards against forgery were also developed. The most impressive chancery product was the papal bull, which takes its name from the lead seal, or* bulla, *used to secure the document and prove its authenticity. Elements of the bull reveal aspects of the development of papal power in the postreform era.*

The bull illustrated on pages 150–51 was issued by Pope Adrian IV (1154–1159) to the monastery of St. Bertin in 1156 to confirm its properties and privileges. The first thing a recipient might appreciate in a bull is the large piece of parchment (animal skin) it is written on. The reproduction here is only a fraction of the real size of the document: bulls measured approximately a foot and a half wide and two feet long.

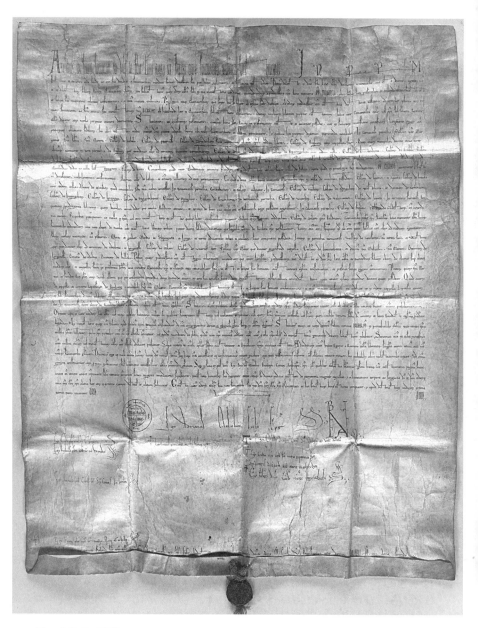

Papal Bull, 1156.

Archivio Segreto Vaticano, Instrumenta Miscellanea 7878. Reproduced with the permission of the Archivio Segreto Vaticano.

Detail of
Papal Bull,
1156.

This means it took most of a whole sheep or goat to make the document. Notice that the text could have been fit onto a much smaller piece of parchment, as there are wide margins and space left between lines. The bull's size was meant to make an impression on the recipient. It communicated the wealth and magnificence of the papacy, while at the same time making the recipient feel important.

The script of the bull was both easy to read and quite elegant. The Latin text of the document was written in a special rhythmic meter called the *cursus,* which made it particularly nice sounding. The document was meant to be read out loud, and the dots that look like periods in the middle of sentences are actually breath marks that show the reader where to pause.

The document is not only signed by the pope himself ("Ego Adrianus catholice eccle eps SS" meaning "I, Adrian, bishop of the catholic church, subscribed"), but also by all the cardinals. Each makes a cross before signing his name, title, and "SS" for subscribed. Here, three cardinal priests have signed (on the left), one cardinal bishop (in the center), and four cardinal deacons (on the right). These signatures were more than just a formality. Gregory VII had tended to rule without consulting the cardinals, and many deserted him during the final stages of his conflict with Henry IV. Gregory's successors were more prudent and collegial: They consulted the cardinals as a body much as an American president consults with his cabinet, and they entrusted cardinals with key positions in the papal government. The signatures of all the cardinals confirmed their active participation in the matter communicated in the bull and their concord with the pontiff. The experience and knowledge of the cardinals in ecclesiastical matters gave continuity to church governance over time.

The bull contains several ornamental elements that also served as safeguards against forgery. The circular design to the left of the pope's signature is called the *rota* (or "wheel"); it contains a cross with the name of the pope below and the names of Saints Peter and Paul, the special patrons of the Roman church, above. In the circle around the cross is a short phrase from sacred scripture that each pope chose as a sort of motto. Adrian's was "OCULI MEI SEMPER AD D[OMI]N[U]M" ("My eyes are ever on the Lord," Ps. 24:15). The monogram to the right of the pope's signature was called the *bene valete,* a Latin salutation used to close papal letters. The lead seal, or bull, was attached to the parchment with silk threads; it included the pope's name and often images of Saints Peter and Paul. The dots used on the round border of the seal and to make the hair and beards of the apostles were fixed in number to try to frustrate forgers.

41

Papal Ceremonial in a Fresco from SS. Quattro Coronati

13th Century

Across the twelfth century, papal ceremonial developed a rich array of new forms and symbols. Just as the administrative developments under Gregory's successors gave the papacy real power to rule, the ceremonial changes in papal ritual achieved the visual splendor appropriate to a monarch. Particularly notable in this process were borrowings from the imperial court in Byzantium. A series of thirteenth-century frescoes in the chapel of San Silvestro at the basilica of SS. Quattro Coronati in Rome drew upon an earlier, ninth-century mythology enshrined in the famous forgery of the "Donation of Constantine." This document purported to be a charter of donation in which the fourth-century emperor Constantine gave the Roman see primacy over all others; endowed the Roman church with all the lands of Rome, of Italy, and of "all the Western regions"; and granted the popes all the ceremonial honors usually reserved for the emperors. It was not unmasked as a pious fabrication until the Renaissance, so eleventh- and twelfth-century popes truly believed they enjoyed these privileges. There is some evidence of popes employing these imperial symbols—such as the wearing of a red mantle—before the eleventh century, but the postreform pontiffs made them regular and highly visible elements in an increasingly elaborate ritual life. This new ceremonial order also dictated particular roles for visitors to the Holy See. The scene depicted here of the emperor Constantine acting as the pope's servant or groomsman, leading his horse by the bridle, was reenacted every year on the fourth Sunday in Lent with the prefect of Rome cast in the servant role, but it was also urged on kings and emperors entering the city (Emperor Frederick Barbarossa refused in 1155). The pope is riding a white horse, which was believed to be an imperial prerogative, and he wears the conical imperial crown or "tiara" supposedly given to Pope Silvester by Constantine, as opposed to the episcopal miters worn by the clerics on the pope's left. Held over the pope's head is another imperial symbol, the baldachin or "ombrellino" (little umbrella). The papal court had the unmistakable "look" of an imperial power by the end of the twelfth century.

Constantine Leading the Pope's White Horse by the Bridle [*Constantino tiene le brigle del cavallo bianco di Silvestro I*].

Reproduced by permission of Scala/Art Resource, N.Y.

42

BERNARD OF CLAIRVAUX

On Papal Sovereignty

ca. 1148–1153

Bernard, abbot of the monastery of Clairvaux, was one of the most influ-
ential men in twelfth-century Europe. His advice was solicited by popes
and kings; his writings on the spiritual life still inspire many today. By
all accounts a mesmerizing speaker, Bernard captivated a cleric in the
service of the bishop of Pisa during a council held there in 1130. This
cleric, Bernardo Pignatelli, accompanied the abbot back to his monastery
and entered the austere life of the reformed Cistercian congregation of
Benedictine monks. Fifteen years later the abbot's protégé was elected
pope and took the name Eugenius III. In the last years of his life
(ca. 1148–1153), Abbot Bernard wrote a work of advice for the pontiff
entitled Five Books on Consideration. *In it he reveals how the papal*
claims to authority that so rocked late-eleventh-century Europe were
broadly accepted by the mid-twelfth century. But he also displays concern
about the growing bureaucracy and pomp of the papal court.

From Book 2, Chapter 8: *The dignity and power of the pope:* Come, let
us still more closely investigate *what* you are, that is to say, the character you represent for a time in the Church of God. Who are you?
The chief priest, the sovereign pontiff. You are the prince of bishops,
the head of the apostles; in priority you are Abel, in government Noah,
as a patriarch you are Abraham, in order Melchisedech, in rank
Aaron, in authority Moses, as a judge you are Samuel, in power Peter,
in virtue of your anointing you are Christ.[9] You are he to whom the

[9] In the book of Genesis (4:4–5), the gifts of Abel, the younger son of Adam and Eve,
were preferred by God to those of his older brother Cain; Noah was builder of the ark
that saved mankind from the deluge (Gen. 6–7); the Gospel of Matthew traces the
genealogy of Jesus of Nazareth back to Abraham; Melchisedech was both king of Jerusalem and high priest (Gen. 14:18–19), and Psalm 110's reference to the messiah being

Bernard of Clairvaux, *On Consideration,* trans. G. Lewis (Oxford: Clarendon Press,
1908), 54–55, 103–4.

keys have been committed, and the sheep entrusted. There are, indeed, other door-keepers of heaven, and other shepherds of flocks, but as you have received both names in a manner different from the rest, so for you they bear a more glorious meaning. Other pastors have each their several flocks assigned to them; to you all the flocks have been entrusted, one flock under one shepherd. . . .

So then, according to your own authorities, other bishops are called to a share in responsibility, you are called to the exercise of plenary power. The power of other men is confined within fixed limits; yours extends to those who have power over their fellows. Have you not power, for sufficient reason, to shut heaven against a bishop, and even deliver him to Satan? Your prerogative, therefore, whether the power of the keys or the pastorate of the flocks, is unassailable. . . .

From Book 4, Chapter 3: *The necessity of curtailing extravagance in dress, &c.:* How is it then with you? Are you not yet awake, and on your guard against those who have surrounded you with the snares of death? Pray bear with me yet a little while. Nay, rather, pardon me when I say these things with less temerity than timidity. I am jealous over you with a godly jealousy, and I would it were as profitable as it is strong. I know where you dwell; unbelievers and subverters are with you. They are wolves, not sheep; but you are the shepherd of these as well as the rest. The consideration will be profitable if it leads you to the discovery of some means of converting them lest they subvert you. They were sheep and turned into wolves; why despair of their turning back again into sheep? Here, here, I do not spare you, so that God may spare you. At least either deny that you are a shepherd over this people, or show that you are. You will not deny it, lest he, whose chair you fill, deny that you are his heir. I mean, of course, Peter, who never, so far as can be ascertained, paraded himself decked with gems, or robed in silks; he was not covered with gold, he did not ride on a white steed, he was not surrounded by soldiers, nor fenced off from his flock by noisy attendants. He thought that without all this he could amply fulfil the salutary command, "If you love me, feed my sheep" (John 21:15). In all this painted pomp you are not Peter's successor, but Constantine's. What I insist on is that while you may toler-

---

"a priest for ever according to the order of Melchisedech" was understood as an affirmation of Christ as priest-king; Aaron, brother of Moses, was the first high priest of the Israelites (Lev. 8); Moses led the Israelites out of bondage in Egypt and received the Ten Commandments from God; after a period of idolatry, Samuel brought the Israelites back to the Lord and "acted as judge over Israel" (1 Sam. 7:6).

ate such pomp and glory to suit the time, you must not claim it as a debt due to you. I rather urge you to consider those things which are a debt due from you. If on state occasions you are robed in purple and decked with gold, I am sure this does not mean that you, the shepherd's heir, shrink from the shepherd's toil, or the shepherd's care; it does not imply that you are ashamed of the Gospel. Albeit, if you willingly preach the Gospel, you, too, have a glorious place among the apostles. To preach the Gospel is to feed the sheep. Do the work of an evangelist, and you have done the work of a shepherd.

"You are advising me," you say, "to feed dragons and scorpions, not sheep." For that very reason, I reply, set about them; but with the word, not with the sword. Why should you again try to use the sword, which you were once for all bidden to put into its sheath? Yet if any one should deny that you have the sword, he does not seem to me to have paid sufficient attention to his Lord's words, "Put back thy sword into the sheath" (John 18:10–11). To you, then, the sword belongs, and it should be unsheathed, it may be with your consent, though not by your hand. Otherwise, if it no way belonged to you, when the apostles said, "Lo, here are two swords" (Luke 22:38), the Lord would not have replied, "It is enough"; He would have said, "They are too many." Both swords belong to the Church, the spiritual and the material; the one is to be used to defend the Church, but the other must even be banished from the Church; the one is wielded by the priest, the other by the soldier, but of course with your consent, and at the command of the Emperor. More of this elsewhere. Now, however, seize the sword which was entrusted to you that you might strike; wound, for the saving of their souls, if not all, if not many even, at all events as many as you can.

43

GARCIA

Criticism of the Papacy:
The Relics of Saints Silver and Gold

ca. 1100?

*Many European observers were much harsher in their criticism of the
new monarchical papacy than was Abbot Bernard. The financial exactions of the papacy were particularly irksome to many, both within and
outside the church. The development of papal government required
resources, and for much of the twelfth century the popes were strapped for
cash. Their traditional sources of income in the city of Rome and the
papal states of central Italy were often impossible to collect due to political upheavals, so the papacy depended more and more on fees generated
by its own bureaucracy and taxes levied on ecclesiastical institutions. The
irony of religious leaders preaching poverty and renunciation to others
but living like princes themselves was not lost on western Christians, and
satirical literature attacking the papacy flourished in the twelfth and
thirteenth centuries. Here is an excerpt from one of the earliest examples.
The author, a cathedral canon of Toledo named Garcia, had visited the
papal court with his archbishop in 1099. The satire turns on the ecclesiastical rite of "translating"—or moving to a new location for veneration—the physical remains ("relics") of saints.*

At the time when Urban, most greedy pontiff of the Roman Church,
translated to Rome the bodies of the most blessed martyrs, Silver and
Gold, collected from the French churches, and while he was interring
them most gloriously with his own hands—as a religious man—in
gold-embroidered purses, Grimoard, archbishop of Toledo, discovered
by chance some of the martyrs' relics. He decided to transfer them
carefully to the shrine of S. Cupidity, and thinking that they would
please the Roman pontiff—for he knew the man's compunction—he
brought them with him to Rome. Now the archbishop was hoping for

---

Tractatus Garsiae or the Translation of the Relics of SS. Gold and Silver, trans. R. M.
Thomson (Leiden: Brill, 1973), 15–21.

the legateship of Aquitaine, granted to the city of Toledo by order of the blessed Gregory in accordance with the ancient privileges of the See. It seemed, on this account, a shame, a crime, that a person of such weight, so plump, so rotund, so delicate, should be denied the dignity held by his predecessors. But, for the rest, although he could drain a full bowl (for he was a brave wine-drinker), although he snored day and night (for he could not keep himself awake,) although he had a true bishop's belly (his distended stomach protruded not a little, since he usually put away a whole salmon at a sitting), although he made it his religious duty to condemn the innocent, persecute the upright, deceive the poor, and cheat orphans of their patrimony by violence, although he took every opportunity to lie (since sometimes he had reason to fear the truth), although, I say, he abounded in these virtues, and in those others which advance the fattest prelates of our time, yet he had no chance of becoming a legate of the Roman Church, unless he presented the Roman pontiff with the precious relics of these martyrs.

Armed with these, since they seemed so necessary, he entered the city of Rome. After praying there in the church of the blessed Peter, prince of the apostles, he went to see Urban. When he had announced himself at the door, he got this response from the doorkeeper: "Whoever wants to see the pope may freely do so—at the introduction of Saint Silver." Hearing this, a Spaniard named Garcia, who by chance had come along with the archbishop, said with a smirk: "Why then is this message not inscribed upon the lintels and doorposts, so that foreign visitors to the pope, seeing the Roman custom in writing, may make it known to the faithful in far-away lands?" As soon as the archbishop had promised Silver, he was admitted to the pope, whom he found seated in a marble alcove, clothed in rich purple, flanked by the plumpest cardinals you ever saw. Four of them held up with their own hands a golden basin of fantastic weight, full of the choicest wine. Out of this the Roman pontiff continually cooled his heated spirits, for his bowels were aflame with an overabundance of various kinds of savouries—he was stuffed to overflowing with these savouries! The cardinals urged him to drink up like a man; and when he had downed a full gallon for the salvation of the world, for the redemption of souls, for the infirm and captive, for the fruits of the earth, for peace, for travellers, for seafarers, and then for the state of the Roman Church, until his swelling belly could take no more, they encouraged him to try a little more, promising to drink along with him. . . . At these words the good Cardinal Gregory of Pavia, who was seated at the lord pope's feet, took in his hand the book which we have heard called

Anticanon or *Exterminator.* From it he read the following homily, to which the Roman pontiff lent an attentive ear, and the cardinals listened closely and approvingly. This was the homily:

O how precious are the martyrs Gold and Silver! How much to be proclaimed! How greatly to be praised! Sinners who possess their relics are perpetually justified, made fit for heaven from being earthly, turned from impiety to innocence. We have seen, we have seen simoniac bishops, sacrilegious, and dissipators of their churches, come to the pope, cleansed with the apostolic blessing on account of these martyrs' relics, no longer enmeshed in crime, not retaining any of their old blame, return home and as if reborn. Whoever, therefore, is infected with an adulterer's lips, whoever is guilty of murder, whoever is polluted with the crime of fornication, whoever is grown pale from the disease of envy, whoever has a perjurer's reputation, in short, all sacrilegious, scandal-mongers, wine-bibbers, thieves, misers, quarrellers, bestial, traitors, contentious, thugs, impious, liars, ill-willed (what more?), all detestable, condemned, infamous, criminals, deportees, sentenced, indeed, all sinners who have offended God in word or deed; let them not hesitate to approach the lord pope bearing the relics of these most precious martyrs, that they may be absolved of all. But without these relics their petition will be in vain.

Sanctity and Just Rulership

44

MANEGOLD OF LAUTENBACH

On Tyranny

ca. 1085

Some have found the first glimmerings of the secular European state in the polemical literature sparked by the investiture conflict. Their evidence comes from extreme supporters of the papacy who had a stake in denying that kings were divinely ordained rulers. Thus, it was the advo-

Manegoldi ad Geberhardum Liber, trans. Brian Tierney, in *The Crisis of Church and State, 1030–1300* (Englewood Cliffs, N.J.: Prentice Hall, 1964), 79–80.

*cates of the theocratic supremacy of the Roman church who first articu-
lated the idea that a mutual pact or covenant governed the relationship
between ruler and people. The Benedictine monk Manegold of Lautenbach (1030–1103) wrote this rationale for the removal of rulers around
1085. It survives in only one manuscript, suggesting that it did not have
a wide circulation and large readership in its time.*

Just as the royal dignity and power surpasses all earthly powers, so
too the man appointed to exercise it should not be base and infamous
but should excel others in wisdom, justice and piety as he does in
place and dignity. It is necessary, therefore, that the one who is to
have charge of all and govern all should display greater virtue than
others and should be careful to exercise the power committed to him
with a fine balance of equity; for the people do not exalt him above
themselves so as to concede to him an unlimited power of tyrannizing
over them, but rather to defend them against the tyranny and wickedness of others. However, when he who is chosen to repress evil-doers
and defend the just begins to cherish evil in himself, to oppress good
men, to exercise over his subjects the cruel tyranny that he ought to
ward off from them, is it not clear that he deservedly falls from the
dignity conceded to him and that the people are free from his lordship
and from subjection to him since it is evident that he first broke the
compact by virtue of which he was appointed? Nor can anyone justly
or reasonably accuse the people of perfidy when it is evident that he
first broke faith with them. To take an example from a meaner sphere,
if a man hired someone for a fair wage to look after his swine and then
found that he was not caring for them but stealing, killing and destroy-
ing them, would not the man withhold the promised wage from him
and remove him ignominiously from his task of caring for the swine?
Now, if this is observed in base things, that a man who does not care
for his swine but destroys them shall not be kept as a swineherd, are
there not just and reasonable grounds for maintaining that, in proportion as humans differ from swine, so too it is more fitting that anyone
who does not strive to rule his subjects but rather to lead them into
error should be deprived of the power and authority over men that he
has received?

45

GUIBERT OF NOGENT

On Royal Powers

ca. 1125

The vast majority of evidence suggests that most twelfth-century Europeans continued to believe that kings were sacred and that monarchs worked to reinforce their connections to holiness. One of the best examples of this is the idea that the royal touch could cure certain diseases, especially the disfiguring malady called scrofula, which was characterized by pus-oozing sores on the face and neck. In the early Middle Ages, kings were not normally accorded miraculous healing powers. Only in the early twelfth century do sources in both France and England begin to claim such powers for monarchs. Guibert, abbot of the monastery of Nogent in northern France, gave the first account of a king "touching for scrofula" in his work On Saints and Their Relics. *Written about 1125, the tract recounts and evinces scepticism about many outlandish stories concerning saints and their relics. But Guibert believed quite strongly in the ability of the saints to work miracles, and he pointed out that God's interventions in our world may sometimes seem mysterious. It is in the context of this discussion that he mentions the healing power of kings.*

There are, I will say, some ambiguous instances to be pondered in which the undeserving on God's left hand seem to receive as much glory as the deserving on His right. For the God who parted the Red Sea for the sons of Israel did the same for Alexander the Great at Pamphylia.[10] Read in Suetonius how the Emperor Vespasian cured a lame man by stubbing his toe on him.[11] Manifest signs have also appeared

[10]Medieval legends about Alexander the Great depicted him receiving miraculous assistance in conquering the port city of Pamphylia on the coast of Asia Minor (modern Turkey).

[11]The Roman author Suetonius included a story in his life of the emperor Vespasian (*De Vita Caesarum* 10.7) in which the ruler cured a lame man by touching the man's leg with his foot.

Guibert of Nogent, *De pigneribus sanctorum,* ed. R. B. C. Huygens, in *Corpus Christianorum Continuatio Mediaevalis* 127 (Turnhout: Brepols, 1993), 90.

at the births of powerful princes, such as the aforementioned Alexander, Julius Caesar, Octavian and others, while portents presaged the deaths of Charles and his son Louis. Even in our own times we have often seen comets appear at the deaths of our own kings or those of the Lotharingians or the English, and at the beginning of reigns.

And what are we to make of the fact that we see our lord King Louis[12] regularly working wonders? With my own eyes I have seen those suffering from scrofula on the neck or elsewhere on their bodies crowd around him seeking his touch, to which he would also add a sign of the cross. I was near the king and even holding the crowd back, but he, with an inborn and serene generosity, motioned with his hand for them to approach, and humbly made the sign of the cross over them. His father [King] Philip also used to zealously exercise the glory of that miracle [of healing], but lost it, through what sins I don't know. I refrain from mentioning what other kings do in a similar manner; but I know that the English king in no way dares to try his hand at such things.

[12]King Louis VI of France (1108–1137), also known as Louis the Fat.

46

EMPEROR FREDERICK I BARBAROSSA

The Canonization of Charlemagne

January 8, 1166

Several kings themselves achieved the status of saints in the twelfth century. The German emperor Henry II (1002–1024) was canonized in 1146; the English king Edward the Confessor (1042–1066) in 1161; and Canute, king of Denmark (1080–1086) in 1165. Emperor Frederick I Barbarossa (1152–1190) even orchestrated the canonization of Charlemagne at his Christmas court at Aachen in 1165. Although the canonization was done by an imperial claimant to the papacy—Pascal III, who was not ultimately recognized as the legitimate pope—subsequent popes never contested the cult, and it flourished.

Monumenta Germania historica, Diplomatum regum et imperatorum Germania 10.2, ed. Henrich Appelt (Hannover: Hahn, 1979), no. 502, 432–33.

In the name of the holy and indivisible Trinity. Frederick, by the favor of divine grace, ever majestic emperor of the Romans. When by divinely ordained grace we originally accepted this pinnacle of ruler-ship in the Roman Empire, it was our foremost desire and intention to follow, in manner of living and ruling, those divine kings and emper-ors who preceded us—especially the great and glorious emperor Charles [Charlemagne]—and, imitating their example, preserve the right of the churches, the well-being of the state, and the integrity of the laws throughout our empire. That Charles, with his whole heart pining after the reward of eternal life, established so many new bish-oprics, built so many monasteries and churches, enriched them with properties and privileges, and made himself resplendent by giving great quantities of alms, not only in these parts but beyond the seas—all in order to expand the glory of the Christian name and propagate the cult of divine religion. These works, and the records of his many and great deeds, more fully manifest [his devotion] than conspicuous belief. In spreading that faith in Christ and in converting barbarian peoples, Charles was a powerful athlete and a true apostle, as the Sax-ons, Frisians, Westphalians, Spaniards, and even Vandals—all of whom he converted to the Catholic faith through the word and sword—bear witness. Even if the sword shall not have pierced the soul, the distress of diverse sufferings, the dangerous struggles, and the daily willing-ness to die in order to convert unbelievers, make him a martyr. Now, indeed, we acknowledge him as a most holy confessor and as among those saved in all eternity, and we venerate him here on earth. We believe him to have lived in a holy manner, to have gone to God in a state of pure belief and true penitence, and to be crowned in heaven as a true and sacred confessor among the holy martyrs. Therefore, boldly inspired by the glorious deeds and merits of the most holy emperor Charles; by the zealous petition of our dearest friend Henry, illustrious king of England; by the persuasive assent and authority of our lord Pope Pascal; and with the counsel of all our princes, both sec-ular and ecclesiastical, we gathered at our annual Christmas court at Aachen for the revelation, exaltation, and canonization of his [Charle-magne's] most holy body. There, at Aachen, his most holy body had been securely buried for fear of hostile foreigners and domestic ene-mies, but it was made manifest by divine revelation for the praise and glory of the name of Christ, for the strengthening of the Roman Empire, and for the well-being of our beloved consort, the Empress Beatrice, and our sons Frederick and Henry. We raised up and exalted that body with great fear and reverence on December 29th in the presence of a great assembly of princes and a copious multitude of clerics and people singing hymns and sacred canticles. . . .

47

The Coronation Rite of Reims
ca. 1230

Although many people before the reform movement counted the anointing of kings among the sacraments of the church, it was excluded from the canonical list of seven sacraments sanctioned by theologians in the twelfth century. But monarchs and their supporters developed a wide array of ceremonies that increasingly emphasized the sacral character of kingship. None was more impressive than the coronation ritual of the kings of France. This liturgical text gives what we might call the "stage directions" for this rite. Composed around 1230, the text is the first to describe the use of the "Holy Ampulla." This was a vial of special chrism popularly believed to have been brought by a dove from heaven when Saint Remigius baptized Clovis (481–511), the first Frankish king to convert to Christianity. Its use in the coronation of French kings is documented from the thirteenth through the eighteenth centuries. (It was smashed in the French Revolution.)

This is the order for anointing and crowning the king. The throne is prepared on a platform projecting somewhat at the edge of the sanctuary and placed in the middle between the choirs where one ascends the stairs and where the peers of the realm, and others if necessary, can be with the king.

. . . The king ought to enter the church accompanied by the archbishops, the bishops, the barons, and others he wishes to bring along.

Ordines Coronationis Franciae: Texts and Ordines for the Coronation of Frankish and French Kings and Queens in the Middle Ages, ed. Richard A. Jackson, 2 vols. (Philadelphia: University of Pennsylvania Press, 1995–2000), 2: 297–305.

Seats should be arrayed around the altar for the bishops and archbishops, with the bishops who are peers of the realm opposite the altar not far from the king and not with too many interspersed between them in an unseemly manner.

Between Prime and Terce,[13] the monks of Saint Remigius ought to come in procession with crosses and candles, bearing the Holy Ampulla, which the abbot should carry most reverently under a silk baldachin supported by four poles carried by monks wearing albs.[14] And when the procession arrives at the church of blessed Denis [near the cathedral] — or at the door of the cathedral if made necessary by the press of the crowd — the archbishop [of Reims] with the rest of the archbishops and bishops and the canons as well, if possible, should go to meet it — or at least with some of the bishops and barons, again, if the press of the crowd outside makes it necessary to limit the number. The archbishop ought to receive the Holy Ampulla from the hands of the abbot, giving a promise to return it in good faith. Then he should carry it to the altar, with the abbot and some of the monks accompanying him, amidst the great reverence of the people. . . .

These things having been completed, the archbishop prepares himself for Mass with the assistance of the deacons and subdeacons, putting on his most distinguished vestments and his pallium.[15] Thus garbed, he processes in the usual manner to the altar. When he arrives, the king should rise up reverently and remain standing.

When, indeed, the archbishop comes to the altar, either by himself or with the other bishops, he ought to ask on behalf of all the churches subject to royal authority that the king promise and confirm by oath that the rights and property of the bishops and their churches will be preserved by him, just as a king should in preserving the realm, et cetera, as is contained in the Ordinary where the three promises and oaths are set out. [In the Ordinary the king recites: "These three things I promise in the name of Christ to the Christian people entrusted to me. First, that the whole Christian people of the church of God may forever be preserved in true peace by virtue of our justice. And that I will prohibit all evils and sins of every kind.

---

[13]*Prime and Terce:* Services in the Divine Office performed just after sunrise and at the third hour after sunrise (approximately 9:00 A.M.).

[14]A baldachin is a cloth canopy; an alb is a long white tunic with long, fitted sleeves.

[15]*pallium:* A special stole of white wool conferred by the pope as a sign of archiepiscopal status.

Third, that I will cultivate equity and mercy in all judgments so that merciful and clement God may reward me and you with his mercy.] Further, the archbishop should administer the oath of the [Third] Lateran Council, namely, to rid his kingdom of heretics. These having been promised and confirmed by an oath sworn on the sacred Gospels, the *Te Deum Laudamus* ["Let Us Praise You, God"] is sung.

Beforehand, the following articles shall have been prepared and placed upon the altar: the royal crown, the sword in its scabbard, the golden spurs, the golden scepter, the staff measuring at least one cubit or more and having ivory above the handhold, the boots woven of purple silk and covered with golden lilies, and a tunic of the same color fashioned after the manner of tunics worn by subdeacons at Mass, as well as a mantle of the same color and style which is made for the most part in the manner of a silk cope, but without a hood. The abbot of Saint Denis in France ought to bring all these things to Reims from his monastery and stay at the altar to guard them.

Standing before the altar, the king puts on these garments. First, his silk tunic and linen shirt, both open more deeply at the chest, in front and behind (namely, between the shoulder blades), with the openings of the tunic closed with silver clasps. Then, the silk boots are put on his feet by the Grand Chamberlain of France; afterwards, the gold spurs are affixed by the Duke of Burgundy and then immediately removed. Next, the king is girded with the sheathed sword by the archbishop, who then draws the sword (placing the scabbard on the altar) and places it in the hands of the king. The king should bear it humbly to the altar and then immediately give it back to the archbishop, who gives it to the Seneschal of France[16] to be carried before the king (until the end of Mass in church and after Mass all the way to the palace).

These things having been completed, and the chrism having been prepared at the altar in a consecrated dish, the archbishop should open the Holy Ampulla over the altar. With a golden needle, he ought to take a small amount of the oil sent from heaven and mix it well with the chrism prepared for the anointing of the king—who alone among all the monarchs of the world enjoys this glorious privilege of being

---

[16] *Seneschal of France:* From the ninth to the thirteenth centuries, the seneschal was the leading royal official in the French court; he was steward of the king's household and could even preside over the court in the king's absence. Concerns about the power of the office led monarchs from the thirteenth century to limit the seneschal to ceremonial roles, like the one described here.

anointed with oil sent from heaven. Then, unfastening the clasps of the openings [in the king's tunic] before and behind, [the king] kneeling on the ground, first the archbishop anoints him with that oil on the top of his head; second, on the chest; third, between the shoulder blades; fourth, on the shoulders; fifth, on the joints of the arms. Then, the antiphon "They anointed Solomon" is sung.

After the clasps of the openings [in the king's tunic] for the anointing are fastened, the purple tunic is put on the king by the Chamberlain of France. Over it, the mantle is draped so that his right hand is free in its opening and over his left it is raised just as the chasuble of a priest is raised.[17] Then the archbishop places the scepter in his right hand and the staff in his left. At last, having called by name all the peers of the realm and with them standing around him, the archbishop takes the royal crown from the altar and he alone places it on the head of the king. Thus crowned, all the peers of the realm, clerical as well as lay, place their hands on the crown and support it from all sides.

With the peers supporting the crown, the archbishop then leads the king thus adorned to the throne prepared for him, draped and decorated with silks, where he places him in the eminent seat so that he may be seen by all. Immediately, the archbishop, having removed his miter out of reverence, kisses the king and after him, all the episcopal and lay peers supporting his crown [do the same]. . . .

[17] *chasuble:* A poncho-like vestment—basically a large, square or circular piece of material with an opening cut in the center for the head so the material draped down over the body. The author is indicating that the king's mantle is to be draped with the clasp at his right shoulder so his right arm rises through the opening and the left arm lifts the cloth of the mantle, showing it to full effect.

48

The Tomb of Edward II
Mid-14th Century

As kings worked to reinforce their claims to holiness, their funerary monuments took on the character of reliquary shrines, and their remains were distributed like those of the saints. The division of royal bodies seems to have begun out of feelings of kinship: Emperor Henry III (d. 1056) ordered that his body be buried next to that of his father at Speyer and his entrails be buried at Goslar where his daughter was

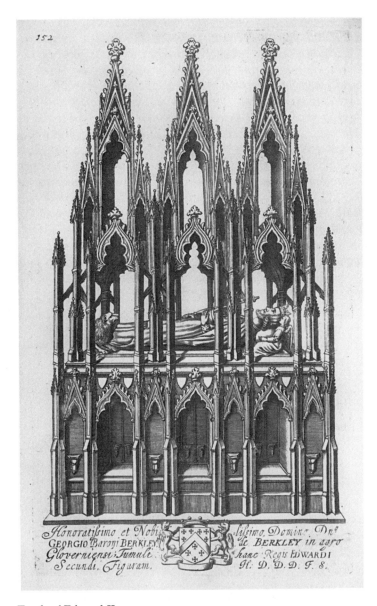

Tomb of Edward II.

From Francis Sandford, *A Genealogical History of the Kings of England* (London: T. Newcomb, 1683). Photo courtesy of the Library of Congress.

interred. The practice took on different connotations, however, in the thirteenth and fourteenth centuries when the French kings had body parts distributed to different churches. When Philip III died in 1285 his corpse was eviscerated and then boiled to disengage the bones. Most of the entrails and flesh were interred in the cathedral of Narbonne, while his heart was given to the Dominican church in Paris, and his bones were laid to rest in Saint Denis. At the same time, royal tombs became more elaborate. That of King Louis VII (d. 1180), placed in front of the main altar of the Cistercian monastery at Barbeaux, had an effigy of the king and adornments of gold, silver, and precious stones. The engraving here shows the funerary monument of the English king Edward II (d. 1327). The king holds a scepter in one hand and the orb in the other. He wears the royal mantle and crown, while a lion, symbol of royal might and majesty, crouches at his feet. Angels support the monarch's head as he gazes heavenward, seemingly transfixed by a vision. The three tiers of gothic arches rising around the effigy invoke the Trinity and form a shape similar to the arklike reliquary chests used to store the remains of saints.

A Chronology of the Origins
and Consequences of the Investiture Conflict
(313–1201)

313	Emperor Constantine (306–337) legalizes Christianity
354–430	Augustine of Hippo
476	Last western Roman emperor deposed
494	Pope Gelasius I (492–496) asserts parity between priesthood (*sacerdotium*) and kingship (*regnum*)
751	Pippin (751–768) becomes king of the Franks with papal approval; anointed by Pope Stephen II in 754
800	Charlemagne (768–814), king of the Franks, is crowned emperor
910	Duke William of Aquitaine founds the monastery of Cluny
962	Otto I (936–973), king of the eastern portions of the Frankish state that become the German empire, is crowned emperor
989–ca. 1040	Peace and Truce of God movement
1024	End of Ottonian dynasty in German empire; Conrad II (1024–1039) founds Salian dynasty
1039–1056	Reign of Emperor Henry III
1042	Peter Damian (1007–1072) writes his life of Saint Romuald
1046	Synod of Sutri; Mathilda of Tuscany born (d. 1115)
1048	Bruno of Toul becomes Pope Leo IX (1048–1054)
1050	Henry IV born
1053	Henry IV crowned king
1055	Victor II (1055–1057) becomes pope
1056	Pataria movement begins in Milan

Henry III dies; Henry IV succeeds to the throne with his mother, Empress Agnes, as regent

1057 Stephen IX (1057–1058) becomes pope

1058 Papal schism with election of both Benedict X and Nicholas II (1058–1061) — the latter recognized as legitimate and consecrated in 1059

1059 Papal election decree

1061 Anselm of Lucca, an advocate of reform, elected pope as Alexander II (1061–1073); opposed by imperial candidate Honorius II from 1061 to 1064

1062 Kaiserswerth coup: Henry IV kidnapped by Archbishop Anno of Cologne, who takes over the regency

1065 Henry IV reaches majority (age fifteen)

1073 Hildebrand becomes Pope Gregory VII; Saxon revolt begins

1075 *March 3–5: Dictatus papae*

June 9: Henry IV defeats Saxon rebels at Homburg

December 8: Gregory's "Admonition" to Henry

1076 *January:* Synod of Worms convened by Henry IV withdraws allegiance from Pope Gregory VII

February 14–20: Roman synod excommunicates Henry IV and declares him deposed

Summer: Saxon princes rebel again

1076– *December–January:* Henry IV goes to Canossa to intercept
1077 Gregory VII and is absolved from excommunication

1077 *March 26:* Rudolf of Swabia elected antiking at Forcheim

1078 *Autumn:* General decree against lay investiture

1080 *Spring:* Decree against lay investiture renewed; Henry IV excommunicated again

June 25: Synod of Brixen called by Henry IV declares Gregory VII deposed; Wibert of Ravenna elected antipope Clement III

October 15: Battle on the Elster: Henry IV defeats antiking Rudolf

1081 Henry IV marches on Rome

1083 *June 3:* Henry IV conquers St. Peter's basilica in Rome

1084 *March 24:* Henry IV and his faction consecrate antipope Clement III in Rome

Summer: Gregory VII calls in his Norman allies to retake Rome; city sacked and Gregory forced to retreat to Salerno

1085 *May 25:* Gregory VII dies in Salerno; succeeded by Victor III (1086–1087)

ca. 1085 Manegold of Lautenbach writes his rationale for the removal of rulers

1088 Pope Urban II elected; in 1089 drives antipope Clement III from Rome

1093 Henry IV's son Conrad rebels against him with papal backing

1095 Pope Urban II calls First Crusade at the Council of Clermont

1099 Pascal II (1099–1118) elected pope

1101 Robert of Arbrissel founds Fontevraud

1105 *December 31:* Henry IV forced by his son Henry V (1105–1125) to abdicate the throne

1106 *August 7:* Henry IV dies

1107 Pope Pascal II reaches agreements with kings of France and England on investiture

1122 Agreements at Worms formally end investiture conflict

ca. 1125 Guibert of Nogent describes royal powers of healing

1148– 1153 Bernard of Clairvaux writes his *Five Books on Consideration*

1161 King Edward the Confessor of England (r. 1042–1066) canonized

1165 Charlemagne and King Canute of Denmark canonized

1170 *December 29:* Thomas Becket killed in Canterbury cathedral

1179 Waldensians seek papal approval of their religious movement

1184 Waldensians, Humiliati, and others condemned as heretics

1201 Pope Innocent III rehabilitates Humiliati, approving their way of religious life

Questions for Consideration

1. Compare the objections to the sexual activity of priests by leaders of the Pataria movement (see Document 6) with those expressed by Peter Damian in his letter to Bishop Cunibert. How are they similar or different?

2. Consider both Humbert of Silva Candida's and Peter Damian's views on simony. Do their views of what happens when a priest is ordained differ? How are priests "holy"?

3. Compare both accounts of the Synod of Sutri. What are the most significant differences, and what do you think accounts for them?

4. Compare the ideas about papal authority that Gregory VII expresses in his letter to Rudolf of Swabia with his later assertions in the *Dictatus papae*. How does Gregory's understanding of the relationship between temporal and spiritual authority seem to differ in these two documents? How might you explain these differences?

5. In his January 1076 response to Gregory's admonition, what precisely are Henry's objections to the pope's behavior and demands?

6. Compare Henry's private letter to Gregory to the public response he circulated in his realm (see Document 21). Are the differences merely rhetorical, or are they substantive?

7. Compare Lampert of Hersfeld's and Gregory VII's accounts of the events that took place at Canossa from December 1076 to January 1077. Are the differences significant? If so, how?

8. Did the agreements reached at Worms in 1122 resolve any of the issues Ivo of Chartres had raised about investiture? What issues were left unresolved? Which of these unresolved issues do you think is most significant, and why?

9. Compare the religious movements of Robert of Arbrissel, the Waldensians, and the Humiliati. What characteristics do they have in common?

10. Is there anything in Gregory VII's letters to Henry IV that suggests he would agree with Manegold of Lautenbach's rationale for removing a ruler?

11. List all of the ways in which the ruler is visually associated with holy things and/or persons in the Reims coronation rite. Is the relationship between power and the holy that is constructed by this ritual different from the relationship communicated in other images of kingship (such as the manuscript illumination of King Dagobert investing Saint Omer or the engraving of the tomb of Edward II)?

Selected Bibliography

PRIMARY SOURCES

Damian, Peter. *The Letters of Peter Damian.* Translated by Owen J. Blum. Washington, D.C.: Catholic University of America Press, 1989.

Gregory VII. *The Register of Pope Gregory VII, 1073–1085.* Translated by H. E. J. Cowdrey. Oxford: Oxford University Press, 2002.

Imperial Lives and Letters of the Eleventh Century. Translated by Theodor E. Mommsen and Karl F. Morrison. New York: Columbia University Press, 1962; reprinted 2000.

Prefaces to Canon Law Books in Latin Christianity: Selected Translations, 500–1245. Translated by Bruce C. Brasington and Robert Somerville. New Haven: Yale University Press, 1998.

GENERAL RESOURCES

Blumenthal, Uta-Renate. *The Investiture Controversy: Church and Monarchy from the Ninth to the Twelfth Century.* Philadelphia: University of Pennsylvania Press, 1988.

Brooke, Z. N. *The English Church and the Papacy from the Conquest to the Reign of John.* Cambridge, U.K.: Cambridge University Press, 1931; reprinted 1989.

Leyser, Karl. "On the Eve of the First European Revolution." In *Communications and Power in Medieval Europe: The Gregorian Revolution and Beyond,* 1–19. Edited by Timothy Reuter. London: Hambledon Press, 1994.

Morrison, Karl F. *Tradition and Authority in the Western Church, 300–1400.* Princeton, N.J.: Princeton University Press, 1969.

Tellenbach, Gerd. *Church, State and Christian Society at the Time of the Investiture Contest.* Translated by R. F. Bennett. Toronto: University of Toronto Press / Medieval Academy of America, 1991.

Tellenbach, Gerd. *The Church in Western Europe from the Tenth to the Early Twelfth Century.* Translated by Timothy Reuter. Cambridge, U.K.: Cambridge University Press, 1993.

Tierney, Brian. "Freedom and the Medieval Church." In *The Origins of Modern Freedom in the West,* 64–100. Edited by R. W. Davis. Stanford, Calif.: Stanford University Press, 1995.

Weinfurter, Stefan. *The Salian Century: Main Currents in an Age of Transition.* Translated by Barbara Bowlus. Philadelphia: University of Pennsylvania Press, 1999.

KEY FIGURES IN THE INVESTITURE CONFLICT

Cowdrey, H. E. J. *Pope Gregory VII, 1073–1085.* Oxford: Clarendon Press, 1998.

Gilchrist, J. T. "Cardinal Humbert of Silva-Candida (d. 1061)." *Annuale mediaevale (Duquesne studies),* 3 (1962): 29–42.

Little, Lester K. "The Personal Development of Peter Damian." In *Order and Innovation in the Middle Ages: Essays in Honor of Joseph R. Strayer,* 317–41. Edited by William C. Jordan, Bruce McNab, and Teofilo F. Ruiz. Princeton, N.J.: Princeton University Press, 1976.

Robinson, I. S. *Henry IV of Germany, 1056–1106.* Cambridge, U.K.: Cambridge University Press, 1999.

ASPECTS OF REFORM

Brooke, C. N. L. "Gregorian Reform in Action: Clerical Marriage in England, 1050–1200." *The Cambridge Historical Review,* 12 (1956): 1–20.

Constable, Giles. "Renewal and Reform in Religious Life: Concepts and Realities." In *Renaissance and Renewal in the Twelfth Century,* 37–67. Edited by Robert L. Benson, Giles Constable, and Carol D. Lanham. Toronto: University of Toronto Press/Medieval Academy of America, 1991.

Cowdrey, H. E. J. "The Papacy, the Patarenes and the Church of Milan." Reprinted in *Popes, Monks and Crusaders.* London: Hambledon Press, 1984, V25–48.

Gilchrist, John. "'Simoniaca Haeresis' and the Problem of Orders from Leo IX to Gratian." In *Proceedings of the Second International Congress of Medieval Canon Law, Boston College, August 12–16, 1963,* 209–35. Edited by Stephan Kuttner and J. Joseph Ryan. Vatican City: S. Congregatio de Seminariis et Studiorum Universitatibus, 1965.

Kuttner, Stefan. "The Revival of Jurisprudence." In *Renaissance and Renewal in the Twelfth Century,* 299–323. Edited by Robert L. Benson, Giles Constable, and Carol D. Lanham. Toronto: University of Toronto Press/Medieval Academy of America, 1991.

Lynch, John E. "Marriage and Celibacy of the Clergy—The Discipline of the Western Church: An Historico-Canonical Synopsis." *Jurist,* 32 (1972): 14–38, 189–212.

Lynch, Joseph H. *Simoniacal Entry into Religious Life from 1000 to 1260: A Social, Economic, and Legal Study.* Columbus: Ohio State University Press, 1976.

Moore, R. I. "Family, Community and Cult on the Eve of the Gregorian Reform." *Transactions of the Royal Historical Society,* ser. 5, 30 (1980): 49–69.

Moore, R. I. "Heresy, Repression, and Social Change in the Age of Gregorian Reform." In *Christendom and Its Discontents: Exclusion, Persecution, and Rebellion, 1000–1500,* 19–46. Edited by Scott L. Waugh and Peter D. Diehl. Cambridge, U.K.: Cambridge University Press, 1996.

Morrison, Karl F. "Canossa: A Revision." *Traditio,* 18 (1962): 121–48.

Remensnyder, Amy G. "Pollution, Purity, and Peace: An Aspect of Social Reform between the Late Tenth Century and 1076." In *The Peace of God: Social Violence and Religious Response in France around the Year 1000,* 280–307. Edited by Thomas Head and Richard Landes. Ithaca, N.Y.: Cornell University Press, 1992.

Robinson, I. S. *Authority and Resistance in the Investiture Contest: The Polemical Literature of the Late Eleventh Century.* Manchester: Manchester University Press; New York: Holmes & Meier, 1978.

KINGSHIP

Bloch, Marc. *The Royal Touch: Sacred Monarchy and Scrofula in England and France.* Translated by J. E. Anderson. London: Routledge & Kegan Paul, 1973.

Kantorowicz, Ernst H. *The King's Two Bodies: A Study in Medieval Political Theology.* Princeton, N.J.: Princeton University Press, 1957.

Reuter, Timothy. "The 'Imperial Church System' of the Ottonian and Salian Rulers: A Reconsideration." *Journal of Ecclesiastical History,* 33 (1982): 347–74.

Spellman, W. M. *Monarchies 1000–2000.* London: Reaktion Books Ltd., 2001.

THE PAPACY

Morris, Colin. *The Papal Monarchy: The Western Church from 1050–1250.* Oxford: Clarendon Press, 1989.

Ullmann, Walter. *The Growth of Papal Government in the Middle Ages: A Study in the Ideological Relation of Clerical to Lay Power.* 3rd edition. London: Methuen, 1970.

Acknowledgments

Acknowledgments continued from p. iv.

"A Letter to Bishop Cunibert of Turin, 1064." From Peter Damian, *The Letters of Peter Damian,* translated by Owen J. Blum in *The Fathers of the Church: Medieval Continuation,* vol. 5, pp. 258–59, 266–69, 270–71, 285. © 1989 The Catholic University of America Press. Used with permission of The Catholic University of America Press, Washington, D.C.

"An Account of Henry's Minority, ca. 1106." From *Imperial Lives and Letters of the Eleventh Century,* edited and translated by Theodor E. Mommsen and Karl F. Morrison, pp. 105–7. © 1962; reprinted 2000 Columbia University Press. Reprinted with the permission of the publisher.

"A Letter to Supporters in Lombardy, July 1, 1073." From *The Correspondence of Pope Gregory VII,* edited and translated by Ephraim Emerton, pp. 11–12. © 1969 Columbia University Press. Reprinted with the permission of the publisher.

"A Letter to Duke Rudolph of Swabia concerning Henry IV, September 1, 1073." From *The Correspondence of Pope Gregory VII,* edited and translated by Ephraim Emerton, pp. 15–16. © 1969 Columbia University Press. Reprinted with the permission of the publisher.

"Admonition to Henry, December 8, 1075." From *The Correspondence of Pope Gregory VII,* edited and translated by Ephraim Emerton, pp. 86–90. © 1969 Columbia University Press. Reprinted with the permission of the publisher.

"Response to Gregory's Admonition, early 1076." From *Imperial Lives and Letters of the Eleventh Century,* edited and translated by Theodor E. Mommsen and Karl F. Morrison, pp. 146–51. © 1962; reprinted 2000 Columbia University Press. Reprinted with the permission of the publisher.

"A Letter to the German Princes, January 1077." From *The Correspondence of Pope Gregory VII,* edited and translated by Ephraim Emerton, pp. 111–13. © 1969 Columbia University Press. Reprinted with the permission of the publisher.

"A Letter to Hermann of Metz, March 15, 1081." From *The Correspondence of Pope Gregory VII,* edited and translated by Ephraim Emerton, pp. 166–75. © 1969 Columbia University Press. Reprinted with the permission of the publisher.

"A Letter to Hugh Candidus, ca. 1084–1085." From *The Letters of Lanfranc, Archbishop of Canterbury,* edited with a facing page English translation from the Latin text by Helen Clover and Margaret Gibson (Oxford Medieval Texts, 1979), pp. 165–67. Reprinted by permission of Oxford University Press.

"The Preaching of Robert of Arbrissel, ca. 1118." From Baudri of Dol, *The Life of Robert of Arbrissel,* chap. 2–3, edited and translated by Bruce L. Venarde in *Robert of Arbrissel (ca. 1045–1116): A Medieval Religious Life,* pp. 12–14. © 2003 The Catholic University of America Press. Used with permission of The Catholic University of America Press, Washington, D.C.

"On the New Knighthood, ca. 1128–1136." From *Bernard of Clairvaux: In Praise of the New Knighthood,* translated by Conrad Greenia, OSCO (Kalamazoo, Mich.: Cistercian Publications, 2000), pp. 45–48. © 2000 Cistercian Publications. Reprinted with the permission of the publisher.

"Visitation to Inspect His Clergy, 1248." From *The Register of Eudes of Rouen,* translated by Sydney M. Brown, edited by Jeremiah F. O'Sullivan, pp. 24, 27. © 1964 Columbia University Press. Reprinted with the permission of the publisher.

"Criticism of the Papacy: The Relics of Saints Silver and Gold, ca. 1100." From *Tractatus Garsiae or the Translation of the Relics of SS. Gold and Silver,* translated by R. M. Thomson, pp. 15–21. © 1973 Brill Academic Publishers. Reprinted with the permission of the publisher.

"On Tyranny, ca. 1085." From Manegold of Lautenbach, *Manegoldi ad Geberhardum Liber,* translated by Brian Tierney in *The Crisis of Church and State, 1030–1300* (Englewood Cliffs, N.J.: Prentice Hall, 1964), pp. 79–80. Used by permission of the translator.

Index

181